GUIDE TO LIFEWORK
Working with Integrity and Heart

GUIDE TO LIFEWORK
Working with Integrity and Heart

A Four-Part Program
To Find Meaning And Fulfillment
In All The Work You Do

Leonard Lang

Published by The Writers' Collective

Published by The Writers' Collective
Cranston, Rhode Island

The suggestions and ideas presented in this book are for general use and are not intended to substitute for individual services provided by qualified professionals.

Jacket design by Dan Ezra Lang for delstudios (delstudios.net)

ISBN: 1-932133-11-9
Printed in the United States of America

Library of Congress Cataloging-in-Publication Data

Lang, Leonard, 1948-
  Guide to lifework : working with integrity and heart ; a four-part program to find meaning and fulfillment in all the work you do / Leonard Lang.
       p. cm.
  ISBN 1-932133-11-9 (alk. paper)
  1. Vocational guidance. 2. Life skills. I. Title.
  HF5381.L313 2003
  650.1-dc21
                          2003000944

Acknowledgements

One of the messages in this book is that the community of people in our lives is essential to realizing anything we want to accomplish. That has certainly been true for me in writing this book. I want to thank participants in my lifework program along with my coaching clients who have been the inspiration for this book in many ways. They were the ones who first suggested I write such a book, and their feedback during classes and coaching sessions helped me refine and develop the model and exercises that are at the heart of this book. Special thanks to those who made it possible for me to offer these lifework programs, especially Tom Smith-Myott who caught on immediately to the spiritual foundation of this work.

I also want to extend my appreciation to everyone who generously volunteered their time and expertise to help get this book into your hands. They are too many to list here, but let me single out for particular thanks Amy Kirkpatrick for helping to make this book more readable from a design standpoint and Paul Eger, Warren Lang, and Marion Lang, who spent time helping me review the entire manuscript—offering large doses of support and encouragement along the way.

Contents

WHERE DO I WORK?

HOW DO I SUCCEED?

Introduction

Welcome to the next 88,000 hours of your work life.

Maybe that's what our first employers should tell us.[1] Maybe then we'd think more carefully about where we're going and how we want to spend that much time.

When you think about how you're going to spend the equivalent of ten years of your life, 24 hours a day, it is easier to recognize that working for a good paycheck isn't going to be enough. It's particularly poignant when people settle for this, even though we live in a society where we are primed to find individual success, where we are blessed with the freedom to choose our work rather than be ordered by the state or by custom, and where we have the educational resources to gain the knowledge and skills we need. Yet so many of us fall into our jobs and careers almost by chance because we have some aptitude for them, rather than because we have a passion and sense of value about the work we do.

---

[1] Multiply 40 hours per week times 50 weeks per year for 2,000 hours per year, multiplied by a career of 44 years (age 21 to 65). That simplification of the yearly number of hours Americans work is supported by "Key Indicators of the Labor Market 2001-2002," a study by the International Labor Organization, which found that Americans were working an average of 1,978 hours per year.

What if there is a better alternative? What if you could wake up feeling eager to get to work? What if you could discover and create a passionate lifework instead of just working all the weeks of your life? What if you could find work that is meaningful to you, work that is in line with your values, that leaves you feeling fulfilled and maybe even joyful in spite of its challenges and stresses? Would that be a better way to spend almost a hundred thousand hours of your time?

If that possibility intrigues you, then welcome to one of the great journeys of your life—the search for meaningful and re-warding work. Feel free to embark on this journey whether you are wondering about switching careers, or are retired and look-ing for volunteer work, or are just starting out looking for your first full-time job.

If you allow it, your journey of discovery will connect you to your deepest passions, dreams, skills, and values and lead you back out again into the world of action and connection with others.

Everyone is on this journey, whether they recognize it or not. Everyone would like to live out their dreams, whether they've abandoned the attempt or not. Everyone must find out how to express who they are in relation to the needs and expec-tations of the world. It's just who we are.

By reading this book you are not only on the journey. You are also choosing to be more active and aware of your journey and the choices you are making to use the 88,000 hours (or the hours you'll have after you retire or the hours you'll have if you are fortunate enough to not need to work for an income). Doing the exercises, you will be clarifying what your vision is for your life, how it fits in with the life of your community, and how you can act to make that vision real. Discovering your vision and doing what you can to make it real—that is what lifework is about. This book is about making that happen. It is brief in or-der to focus only on what you really need to succeed.

Some people are very fortunate about work. Their journey toward a unique vision may be fraught with difficulties, but at least they know their destination at a very young age. They had a vision about their lifework and pursued it. Everyone who knew one of my nephews from the time he was two knew he would be a visual artist. His drawings of fish and dragons were delightful and impressive at that early age, and he took to it with great intensity and focus. At his high school graduation, in the mosaic of photographs shown in a slide show of the graduating class, there was a picture of him at about three years old in a smock, holding a paint brush in front of an easel, looking pleased with himself and the world. It fit him at 3. And you could take that same picture of him today in his studio where he's still painting with pleasure, though these days he's also designing CD jackets and often using his computer for graphics.

Let's look at another photo. In it a child is standing at a chalkboard in first grade writing the sentence, "I want to be a doktor." That's just what he became. I once interviewed this physician, and he told me he had no idea how he came to this decision since none of his relatives were physicians, nor had he experienced any particular life-altering medical event in his young life, but at age six right up through his current practice he knew this was his destiny.

Most of us need a little more assistance moving forward on our journeys. Between the covers of this book, you'll find that assistance. The tools and resources presented here have been tested and developed in years of practical workshops attended by engineers and artists, high school graduates and Ph.D.s, retirees and people in mid-career, teens and seniors, software developers and store owners—all seeking meaningful careers, just like you.

Completing the step-by-step exercises will help you do what you love and express who you are, to live by your values, to develop yourself, and to contribute to others.

To succeed in this work, you won't need to grit your teeth or display unusual reserves of willpower and determination. Instead, you'll be relying on your own dreams and vision to energize and motivate you. When you discover and accept your personal vision of meaningful and joyful work, your desire to accomplish it will be more powerful than any willpower you can muster.

You'll be encouraged and helped to locate the values you hold that will most help you on this journey. And you'll be helped through the hard times as well. Some of you may have tried to make changes in your life before and run into difficulties that stumped you. Similarly, no matter how brilliant your lifework plan, no matter how motivated and excited you are, you may bump into moments of discouragement here as well. You may find the world doesn't respond to your dreams as you expected or as quickly as you hoped. That's why this book also includes the keys to successfully dealing with setbacks so you don't become so discouraged that you abandon your plans or act as if you are helpless.

A note on how to use this book. This is a four-part program. Following the exercises in order, chapter by chapter, will move you most logically and quickly from your impulses to your vision to your action plan and success. But feel free to focus on what is most relevant to you now, while not avoiding something just because it seems scary or difficult. Not every exercise will prove appropriate for everyone, but if you're not sure of an exercise, give it a try, and enjoy the journey.

Chapter 1. Getting Started

When have you totally loved your work? Can you recall any time when—in spite of all the stresses, all the deadlines, all the hours, all the challenges—you felt a deep sense of satisfaction? A moment when the work seemed meaningful, fulfilling, even joyful and just flowed along so that you barely noticed the time? Perhaps you sweated through the night with a group on completing a report. Or maybe you reorganized office space that had hindered everyone's work. Or you solved that tricky equation or eliminated that software glitch that had stumped you for so long. Or you lost yourself completely in your music. Or maybe you helped warring parties in your office reach an understanding. Or maybe you felt it everyday as a cashier as you boosted people's spirits with a kind word, a personal connection, a welcome joke. Or you might have volunteered—helping at a soup kitchen, tutoring a student, assisting a senior with a home repair, or sitting with someone in the hospital.

Most people can recall at least a few such experiences. But for far too many, those experiences are occasional. They come and go, while everyday work is too often de-energizing and frustrating—a world apart from our values, our spiritual lives, and our passions.

This lack of satisfaction with our daily work, unfortunately, is only the beginning. Along with the frustration comes significant mental and emotional stress. According to one study, those who reported high levels of job strain also scored high for depression, anxiety, and hostility.[2] This in turn can lead to physical problems and even death. I often ask my lifework classes what hour is the most deadly in our society. Most people get it right. It's between 8 and 9 am Monday morning when most cases of heart attack occur.[3,4] In Japan, where April is the peak business season, that's also when there is the greatest number of sudden deaths, according to another study.[5]

In short, work is literally killing us, and the warning signs start early with the killing of our spirits.

I once saw a sign above an employee's desk that summed it all up: "This is a test. It is only a test. If this had been a real job, you would have received raises, promotions, and other signs of appreciation."

But it doesn't have to be that way. Work can truly be a means of living instead of a cause of death. It can be a place for fulfilling one's dreams, for expressing one's creativity, and for serving in ways we find meaningful. We can receive raises, promotions, and signs of appreciation. That is, we can have adequate financial support to meet our physical needs and many of our material interests, as well as meeting our emotional needs for support and esteem. That in turn will help our health. When we feel life is meaningful, our perception of our health improves, as do the objective measures of our health.[6] That's all wonderful, but today we can expect even more. We can set our sights on joy, fulfillment, and meaning through our work.

---

[2] *Archives of General Psychiatry*, June 1997
[3] James Muller, "Circadian Variation in Frequency of Sudden Death," *Circulation Journal*, Jan 87.
[4] Christopher Martyn, "Hebdomadal Rhythms of the Heart" *British Medical Journal*, Dec. 23, 2000, contains references to a number of related studies.
[5] *European Heart Journal*, 1999;20:338-343.
[6] Idler and Kasl, *Journal of Gerontology*, 1991—Vol. 46, no. 2, pp. 655-665.

Right Action, Right Work

In India people have traditionally used the term *dharma* to talk about one's path in life. Dharma can be literally translated as "right action," but it is often used to describe what one was put on earth to do. We can speak of being in one's dharma or acting according to one's dharma. The opposite is trying to be something you're not, living someone else's dharma.

The Bhagavad-Gita, Hinduism's most beloved sacred text, notes that it is better to serve well in what might be considered a lowly occupation if that is your dharma than try to take on a princely one if that is not. (Obviously this can be abused if *someone else* is telling you you're the street sweeper and they're the millionaire. Then it's no longer a spiritual fact, but a political act.) In the West, we have a different term, *calling*. In the Bible, people are often called to do something. In the New Testament we hear of Paul on the road to Damascus literally being called by God to a new path, as was Mother Teresa in starting her life among the most disenfranchised.

But calling doesn't only apply to those in religious orders. We each have a calling (or more than one over the course of a life). As Mother Teresa said, "I am holy the way I am holy; you have to be holy the way you have to be holy."[7]

We must each find our own path, our own dharma, our way to discover and use our unique gifts and passions, our own calling. The term calling is so often associated only with clergy, that I prefer the term lifework. The central work experience of your life. When you're living your particular dharma, or listening to your calling, or working in your vocation, or doing your lifework—however you want to describe it—you are likely to experience your life as meaningful and fulfilling.

---

[7] Ann Petrie, Richard Attenborough, Mother Teresa, *Mother Teresa*, a documentary originally released by Petrie Productions, Burlingame, California, 1986.

Signs and Guides

While there is no personality test or diagnostic exam that can tell you if you are doing your lifework, there are guideposts or indicators that can help you.

- You feel passionate about your lifework.
- You feel a sense of joy about your lifework.
- You feel energized by your lifework.
- You are aligned with your fundamental beliefs and values.
- You are using and developing your gifts and skills.
- You are helping others by what you do.
- You are feeling connected—to yourself, to others, to whatever you think of as Divine or a spiritual center.

In one of my earlier careers I wrote profiles—of physicians, entrepreneurs, artists. Whether the person was a poet or an administrator, they tended to say the same thing: "I'm excited when I wake up each morning." Or, "I can't believe people pay me to do this. It's what I'd do for nothing." Or, "I never feel like I'm working." "I'm so grateful to be doing this for my work. It's so rewarding."

This doesn't mean they weren't working in difficult and what most of us might call stressful circumstances. For instance, I interviewed many physicians. Some were neurosurgeons whose slightest error could destroy a person's brain, and some were ER physicians working 12-hour shifts and making rapid life and death decisions daily. But they were doing what they most loved to do—the first key to successful lifework, and a good indicator that the other indicators were also in place. It's hard to be passionate over time if you aren't using your skill, if you don't feel you are making a meaningful contribution to others, and if you are out of touch with your values, beliefs and spirituality.

By contrast, an ABC/Wall Street Journal poll [8] found that half of Americans would choose a different career if they could. I'd argue many of them *could* choose a new career, if they knew how. In fact, I see such changes all the time in workshops I hold in colleges, churches and other organizations, in coaching sessions and coaching support groups I lead.

EXERCISE 1: Setting Goals

Purpose
- [ ] To clarify why you are reading this book and to begin goal setting

What You Need
- [ ] The worksheets that follow (3 Goals and My Dream Goal)
- [ ] Pen or pencil
- [ ] 15 minutes

Note: Although worksheets are provided after each exercise, you may prefer to keep some or all your notes and exercise responses in a hard copy or computer lifework journal (see Exercise 18 on creating a lifework journal).

What To Do
1. Decide on three goals you have in using this workbook. Be honest. Perhaps your goal is just to tickle your imagination about work, which would mean you will do exercises until you have some new ideas and dreams. Maybe it's to force yourself to review where you are. Maybe it's to find a new dream career. But what do you actually want to have happen by the time you have finished all the exercises. (If you feel uncertain, then put down your best "guesses" as a kind of working hypothesis.)

2. Now determine when you will complete each of these goals. Not a menacing deadline, but what I prefer to call a *lifeline*, a date that's pulling you toward success. Not something im-

---

[8] *World News Tonight*, "Wall Street Journal/ABC News Poll," ABC, New York. April 15, 1998.

posed from the outside, but a time when you would like to have accomplished these goals and feel it is reasonable to do so if you are committed to this work. Can this date change if you need it to? Of course. But whether you are very deadline driven or very uncomfortable with deadlines, you will probably benefit from having something to motivate and remind you.

3. Let someone know about these three goals and deadlines. Choose someone you trust. Tell them they don't have to do anything about these goals and deadlines except be aware of them. The very act of communicating to others what your goals are begins to move your ideas into the world and usually sets up a sense of responsibility about accomplishing them—even if the other person doesn't remind you.

Worksheet: 3 Goals

3 Goals	Completion Dates

4. Review the three goals. Now dream a little. If you are like many people, you might secretly like to accomplish something even bigger by the time you finish these exercises and readings, something that you don't want to quite admit to yourself, let alone to someone else. Often we have big dreams that we don't want to admit because we want them so much and feel we will be hurt when we don't get them. Here's a chance to at least admit to yourself a big goal you may have.

Worksheet: My Dream Goal

Class participants sometimes surprise themselves when completing this assignment. One man came up with three goals about writing. When asked to look for the larger dream or goal, he realized he wanted to buy a farm where he could best do this writing, a scary idea that seemed too big. Challenging himself to complete this goal, he started taking actions he hadn't dreamed of just a few days earlier, including looking for land he might buy, checking on mortgages, and reviewing his finances. If you don't admit your dream, it has almost no chance of happening. If you do, you can begin to enjoy the excitement of working toward what you most want, even if you can't bring yourself to tell someone else about it...just yet.

Your Unique Vision

Why aren't you following your lifework dreams right now? One likely reason is that you don't know or don't think you know what that lifework is. Why not? After all, you have probably thought about your life many times in many ways over the years, in fact, since childhood when you might have imagined yourself the next Albert Einstein, Michael Jordan, Georgia O'Keefe, Neil Armstrong, Maya Lin, Bill Gates, Margaret Thatcher, Toni Morrison, Malcolm X, or whoever your favorite person was.

But somewhere along the way, we learned we couldn't be political heroes, sports stars, rock stars, acclaimed authors, revolutionary painters, breakthrough inventors, billionaire entrepreneurs, or scientific geniuses. We learned that lesson well. All too well. By the time we enter the work world, most of us have learned to become "realistic," meaning most of us have learned to compromise before we even tried out our dreams. We've learned to be embarrassed about our own big dreams that seem to others foolish and impossible. We learn to abandon our vision or at least put it off in order to make money and be conventionally productive in the world.

That's unfortunate. Doing work just to make a buck or get started is not a vision. Let's be clear about this. It can be useful to make an apparent detour from our dreams. We might work at an entry-level position at a fast food restaurant or as the assistant to someone's assistant. It can be appropriate to take up work that isn't your passion—if it's a first step toward your vision or if it helps you take a financial step on the way to achieving that vision. It's necessary in many cases to put aside some money in order for you and your family to be secure enough to really go after your vision later. But is that what you are doing? Or have you just become "realistic" and deeply unfulfilled in the process, giving away not only your life dreams but also your gifts that could be used so much more powerfully to help others as well as yourself?

To look honestly at what your lifework might be and to succeed in this journey, you need a vision for your life.

"Without vision, the people perish," according to the Book of Proverbs in the Bible. One way to read this is to recognize that when a group (Democrats, Baptists, environmentalists, etc) doesn't have a vision, there is nothing to motivate or unite them, nothing that really defines them and binds them. Eventually they will dissolve or be assimilated into other groups that do have a motivating vision. The quote is true on a deeper level as well. Something else perishes as well without a vision. There is also a death of the spirit when there is no sense of purpose and vision, no sight of where you are to go. The same is true for individuals. With no vision, it is hard to sustain action that feels meaningful. There is a tiredness and dullness of spirit.

According to psychologist and author John Welwood, "All significant achievements come about through vision and intention. No one—whether an artist, a mountain climber, a yogi, or an entrepreneur—can persist in a long, arduous undertaking without a vision of what he or she wants to realize."[9]

And we need to believe in ourselves and our vision. The power of vision and commitment can be astounding. As a young member of the African National Congress, before he became a political prisoner for 27 years, Nelson Mandela of South Africa announced that he would become the first black president of South Africa. This was an outrageous claim that many leaders in his own party thought was naïve and arrogant. After all, the country was locked in a stubborn apartheid system with no signs of it weakening, let alone collapsing. And even if Mandela were to live long enough to see his people freed from this official discrimination, what was to say that he would be the one chosen to be president? There were many other established and up-and-coming leaders in the black community of South Africa. Yet, his prediction came true, and Mandela became his nation's first post-apartheid and first black president, inspiring the world and leading his country into a new era of democracy.

Because of his unusual and painful struggle, it may seem that Mandela's story is not relevant for us everyday folks who are not expecting to lead a nation after decades in jail. However, it can give us pause when we want to say our own dreams are ridiculous, unrealistic, impossible, or downright foolish.

Life's Questions

There are many ways to discover and develop your vision and commitment. In this book we are going to break it down into just three fundamental questions you'll need to answer:

1. **Who** am I?
2. **What** is my purpose, given who I am?
3. **Where** do I work to accomplish my purpose?

---

[9] John Welwood, Love and Awakening: Discovering the Sacred path of Intimate Relationship, (New York, HaperCollinsPublishers, 1996), p. 3.

Three questions. None require you to get another degree or find a mentor or expert or search the four corners of the globe. In fact, you have the answer to these three questions within your experience and feelings and knowledge. Of course, others can and will help you on this journey in many ways, but ultimately, only you know what you need to be doing. Only you know what feels right and meaningful and fulfilling.

Answering these three questions will generate your vision. But that's only half the work. How many times have you heard someone say, "I had that idea before those entrepreneurs who developed it, or before that inventor invented it?" Maybe it was a flavor of ice cream, or maybe it was a way to tackle an epidemic. And maybe they really did come up with the ideas first. But their ideas weren't put into action. Put simply–without action, nothing happens. Don't act, and you don't even survive. So once you have a vision, you need to act, and to act wisely and consistently over time. For this, you need some form of action plan. To begin the action plan you need to start answering a fourth question:

4.   **How** can I succeed?

Three Ws and an H. Who, What, Where and **How.**

The rest of this workbook is divided into sections to answer each of these questions in turn.

WHO AM I?

Chapter 2. Your Unique Gifts

In order to answer who we are for the purposes of lifework, we need to understand three areas of our lives:
- Our resources and skills (our gifts)
- Our passions
- Our values and beliefs.

Let's start with resources and skills. These include what we have been given in this life along with the additional abilities and qualities we have developed.

What we have been given may include: wealth, loving parents, a healthy body, good education, a brilliant mind, a love of beauty, a sensitive nature, a sense of confidence, an ability to connect with people. Along with the unique combination of personal gifts (which we will examine later), I believe we all share at least some degree of key *universal* qualities or abilities which we can use, ignore, or abuse.

They include:
- Honesty
- Courage
- Persistence
- Curiosity
- Energy and enthusiasm
- Compassion

We need to draw on all of these universal gifts to succeed in our lifework process. The one we need to begin this work is *honesty*. What philosophy, religion, psychology does not praise the value of honesty? Or as that inscrutable philosopher Groucho Marx put it, "The secret of life is honesty. If you can fake that, you've got it made."

While we can all think of situations where some dishonesty might be acceptable (white lies when the truth creates pointless suffering over a small matter such as telling our children Santa is real), it is hard to imagine being dishonest with ourselves and succeeding. To know ourselves we must be honest. To know what we most want out of life, what vision propels and inspires us, we must be honest.

Sometimes being honest with ourselves isn't easy. In fact, it can be painful. It hurts to notice our apparent failures or limits. It hurts to admit we deeply want something which we aren't sure we can ever have. We know this since we were children when we wanted a parent's attention and it wasn't there, or when we wanted a certain toy or to be included with a set of friends and it didn't happen. Maybe we wanted to be professional musicians or sports stars and that hasn't happened. So we may have learned to pretend that we didn't really want it. It can seem easier to lie to ourselves and say, "Whatever," or to tell ourselves we don't really care about a job, a romantic partner, owning a house, or embarking on a trip or adventure. In the long run, that's really not easier as our frustration builds, and we wonder what we are missing from our lives.

To be honest in the face of challenges and disappointments we need the next universal quality—*courage*. We need courage to look at what we want and what obstacles we might face. Courage can help us save lives—other people's or our own. Helping us to find the courage we need is our innate drive to be happy and to lead fulfilling lives that feel meaningful. We may have to face the resistance or anger of people we are close to, such as parents, spouses, or friends. They may not want us to give up the six-figure income to pursue a lower paying career, or may not show the faith in our abilities we'd like. But courage keeps us going.

We are also pushed into courage at times by our losses and despair, or rather the realization that things have become so painful, it becomes absolutely necessary to take action. This is what people often talk about when hitting bottom. However scary an action may seem, it can't be worse than the painful condition we are already experiencing.

Courage keeps us going through major obstacles while the quality of *persistence* keeps us going through everyday obstacles and in spite of our impatience about achieving results. All of us find ourselves pursuing something doggedly at one time or another in our lives, demonstrating our capacity to persist. Maybe we are persistent in solving car problems, or resolving conflicts, or coming up with money to take a trip. Thinking about your life you'll probably find some, most likely many, areas where you have been *honest* with what you wanted, had the *courage* to face obstacles and shown *persistence* in achieving them. Such persistence may have led to success for you, as it has for so many people. Edison persisted in his dream of a reliable electric light even after 10,000 unsuccessful attempts (which he regarded as 10,000 successes in learning how not to make a light bulb). The same trait is needed in the case of lifework.

Helping you to persist is the **energy and enthusiasm** that comes with the territory when you pursue something you really love. That also brings with it the necessary **curiosity** about the field and how to get there.

Finally, we all share a fundamental ability to understand the suffering of others, the ability to empathize and be compassionate. **Compassion** for others means we are willing to do what we love in service to others. Compassion for ourselves is just as important and allows us to accept our failings and faults without overwhelming ourselves with our shortcomings and destroying our desire and ability to act. According to Nobel Laureate, His

Holiness the Dalai Lama, the one thing that is always good for ourselves and for others is compassion.

Next, you are going to do an exercise that will help you connect with those times in your life where you succeeded and exhibited some or all of these universal gifts.

EXERCISE 2: Building on Success

Purpose
- ❏ To reconnect with success in your life
- ❏ To understand your personal process for success in order to build upon it

What You Need
- ❏ Two Building on Success worksheets that follow
- ❏ Pen or pencil
- ❏ 20 minutes

What To Do
1. Take a moment to list a few times in your life when you succeeded in something that was important to you. It can be something that now seems unimportant or something that's changed your life.
2. Then review the example on the next page, which shows how someone might have exhibited honesty, courage, etc. in small but valuable ways.
3. Using the following worksheet, take one of the situations you thought about in instruction number 1. Write down the goal and how you exhibited honesty, courage, etc.
4. Do this one more time with another example from your life.

Building on Success Worksheet
Example

GOAL
Try out for community theater.

Honesty
I admitted I wanted it, though I knew it wasn't something others considered important and that I might fail.

Courage
I told others and auditioned for the part I most wanted.

Persistence
I practiced in front of a mirror repeatedly and asked friends to critique me.

Curiosity
I found out what the director was looking for. I asked friends for feedback.

Energy
I got excited about performing and showed that feeling to the director.

Compassion
I took this risk without making it about being a good or bad person. I also helped another auditioner to relax.

Building on Success Worksheet

GOAL

Honesty

Courage

Persistence

Curiosity

Energy

Compassion

Building on Success Worksheet

GOAL

Honesty

Courage

Persistence

Curiosity

Energy

Compassion

Skills, Talents, Personal Gifts

In addition to universal qualities, we each have a unique combination of particular, individual skills and experiences which help make us who we are and help us work toward our fulfillment and the betterment of our world.

These gifts draw on universal qualities like compassion and energy but are more specific, such as the skill of writing clearly or working with wood or relating well to young children or inventing products.

In my programs, I find that people tend to underestimate their skills and talents. It's something we all do to some extent. We may not recognize skills that aren't rewarded or noticed. For example, we may not realize how good we are at organizing people, though family members and colleagues automatically turn to us when beginning some new task. It's not part of our job description and not something our family thinks much about, but it's an invaluable ability. We also tend to ignore talents that have lain dormant for years, such as being able to play an instrument, sketch faces, fix machinery, grow plants, or calm down people during crises.

Or we may acknowledge a skill, but discount it as trivial or irrelevant to our career dreams. We may know we can sight read music, but say to ourselves that this is of no value since we are not going to perform music as our lifework. But it can sometimes be very revealing to see all that we are as skilled human beings, to get the full picture in order to make new connections. We may realize that sight reading music is part of an ability to image things and transform them into another sense, which might be useful in working in a host of creative enterprises, whether inventing products or developing ad campaigns.

Taking stock of skills can be a daunting task. It's hard to know where to start. Sometimes trying to think of everything leads to thinking of nothing because it's so overwhelming. I know when people ask me to list the best books I've ever read or favorite movies, I think of one or two and then go blank—not because that's the end of it but because I don't have a good way to focus. So it might help in this case to break down our skills and talents into different areas.

Howard Gardner's Multiple Intelligences

One way to break down skills into meaningful categories is to look at what Harvard educator Howard Gardner calls multiple intelligences. He has come up with seven of them. There can be something electric about reviewing these intelligences and realizing that you have many kinds of expertise that maybe you (and others) haven't credited yourself with possessing.

The seven intelligences are:

Visual/Spatial
Forming and using mental images
Verbal/Linguistic
Applying language skills—listening, speaking, writing
Musical/Rhythmic
Recognizing and working with musical patterns and sounds
Logical/Mathematical
Working with inductive/deductive reasoning, working with numbers
Bodily/Kinesthetic
Knowledge, use, and movement of the body
Interpersonal
Communicating with others, showing empathy
Intrapersonal
Reflecting on self and one's thinking processes and emotions

Take a moment now to reflect on each area. Then jot down any thoughts about skills or talents you may have in each area. This will help stimulate your thinking for the next exercise, which will use the Examples of General Skills which follows:

Examples of General Skills

Build things	Collaborate with others
Come up with fresh ideas	Complete projects
Compose music	Create vision
Develop training sessions	Do scientific research
Empathize with others	Energize/motivate others
Explain things in writing	Explain things verbally
Find information	Handle details
Heal others	Initiate projects
Lead teams	Listen
Manage projects	Organize others
Paint/Draw	Play a musical instrument
Play with children	Play with animals
Program computers	Provide useful feedback
Remember	Repair things
Resolve/mediate conflicts	Sculpt
Show patience to others	Solve interpersonal problems
Solve computer problems	Speak publicly
Synthesize ideas	Train others
Understand new situations	

EXERCISE 3—Personal Skills Inventory

Purpose

❏ To recognize those particular skills (innate talents, developed skills) that make you who you are. These are also the key skills you can bring to bear on the lifework process.

What You Need

❏ Personal Skills Inventory Worksheet or paper divided into three columns

❏ Pen or pencil

❏ 20–30 minutes

What To Do

1. List in the left column, your top 10 to 15 skills, whether you use them a lot or not, whether they are your favorites or not.

Remember to include skills you use in nonwork settings as well as at work (as in the sample inventory). Use the Examples of General Skills to help stimulate your thinking, as well as the list you made from Gardner's multiple intelligences.

2. List in the second column examples of where you have used the skill (just brief notes to remind you).

3. In the final column, break down, when possible, each general skill into its component skills as shown in the sample list.

4. Star or highlight the top five component skills according to what you feel you enjoy a great deal.

Look for patterns. Look for underlying similarities. For instance, in the sample list that follows, as varied as the major skills seem to be, the idea of listening for key ideas occurs in each of the skill areas. By interviewing people and/or listening to them, the person was able to design a living room, develop a lesson plan, create software, and write profiles—very different outcomes, but all of them involving creativity and listening. If the interviewing and listening skills are the starred skills, then this person may want to find a lifework where that is central to his or her everyday activities.

Remember to include skills you love to use and have only used on rare occasions. They may be the ones you now most want to pursue.

Sample Personal Skills Inventory

SKILL	Example	Details
Remodel houses	Designed and constructed new living room for son	-Listened to son's needs -Created new layout -Communicated it through drawings -Developed practical construction plans -Did drywalling and painting as part of team
Teach kids	Taught Sunday School for 4th–6th graders	-Created lesson plan based on what committee suggested -Led classes -Talked with parents about their children
Develop software	Senior developer for a medical device manufacturer	-Interviewed users about software needs -Analyzed information from users -Designed systems based on analysis -Coded, tested software -Trained staff to use software -Deployed software
Edit and write technical and related articles	Edited medical staff newsletter for HMO	-Developed story ideas -Managed staff of writers -Checked articles for accuracy and clarity -Interviewed physicians -Wrote profiles

Worksheet: Personal Skills Inventory

SKILL	Example	Details

Worksheet: Personal Skills Inventory

SKILL	Example	Details

Chapter 3. Your Passions

My name is Leonard Lang. Am I an author? A teacher? A man? A human being? A learner? A tiny movement in the great fluctuating ocean of life? An energy field with a certain vibration? A good guy? An uncle, a brother, a son, a loser, a winner?

Am I all of these things or none of them?

Who am I can be a silly or profound question. It is sometimes used as a mind-stumping meditation question by Zen students, urging them into ever-deeper levels of themselves and beyond all temporary definitions of self.

In the context of lifework, *who am I* can be seen practically as a way of finding out what moves us most in life, what makes me, *me* and what makes you, *you*—without which you feel life is not quite meaningful or fulfilling. Who am I is about what is essential to the full expression of your spirit, your soul, your core, authentic self.

To learn that, you need to know what your passions are. If you discover what they really are, you can move ahead very powerfully in your journey toward achieving your lifework. You can act from your essential self by expressing the deepest passions and values which arise from the indescribable depth of ourselves.

You could just list your passions. But I've found that it's more helpful and generally satisfying to organize your passions with a greater sense of wholeness and connection. A good way to do that is to use the technique of mindmapping®.

Mindmapping, developed by Tony Buzan, is a marvelous way to brainstorm while connecting factors that might otherwise seem disjointed. It's more fun, colorful, and playful than simple brainstorming and is designed to use more of our brain. It is also quite simple. (Use the mindmap at the end of the directions as a reference.)

EXERCISE 4: Your First Passions Mindmap

Purpose
❑ To reconnect with those things you love by brainstorming about them
❑ To define your many passions in a few words
❑ To organize your main passions in a simple, clear format
What You Need
❑ The Example of a Passions Mindmap that follows the instructions
❑ Unlined sheet of paper or the Passions Mindmap Worksheet that follows the instructions
❑ Pens or markers in a variety of colors
❑ 15–20 minutes
What To Do
1. Place the paper in landscape mode, meaning it appears wider than it is tall. In the center of your paper write the words *My Passions* using any color(s) you like.
2. Next to the words, draw and color some picture that signifies to you the topic, in this case, your passions.
3. It may be something symbolic such as a heart with lightning flying out of it into a blue sky. Or it may be abstract shapes like a doodle. Or you may like to draw figures doing activities you most love. The only rules here are to let yourself go and to keep it simple. Don't try to be all-inclusive. The picture need not win any art awards (my classes always relax af-

ter they see some of the inscrutable images I produce). It simply has to signify for you, your passions.

4. Now you have the words My Passions and the drawing that represents those passions. Enclose these words and your drawing in a circle, oval, or similar shape.

5. Radiating out from this oval, print a single keyword representing a passion, and underline that word so that the line is attached to the inner oval. For example, a passion might be music. Another might be nature. Another might be history. Another might be friends. There will probably be some overlap between these categories, as between friends and nature. That's fine. Feel free to draw pictures or images that represent those passions, such as a sketch of a piano or of notes for the music.

6. Add sub-branches with keywords. For instance, after writing music, you can draw additional branches from the main music branch to define what you mean by your passion of music. For example, you may have a branch labeled playing music and one labeled listening (see the example that follows). The listening branch in turn can break up into branches labeled classical and jazz. The jazz branch may then break up into music from the 1920s and swing. Keep all these sub-branches in the same color as the main branch.

Some people tend to dismiss activities, especially their work activities if they know they don't like their work. Yet there are probably some activities at work that they love. For instance, you may dislike your job as a computer programmer, but you do enjoy meeting with your creative team and leading them into new ideas or solving problems. That's important to note, even though you are dying to get out of a particular job or field.

The point is to get them down on the page in some connected manner. You can redo your mindmap later to reorganize it or to add or subtract branches. So don't worry if it's not perfectly organized or complete right away.

Example of a Passions Mindmap

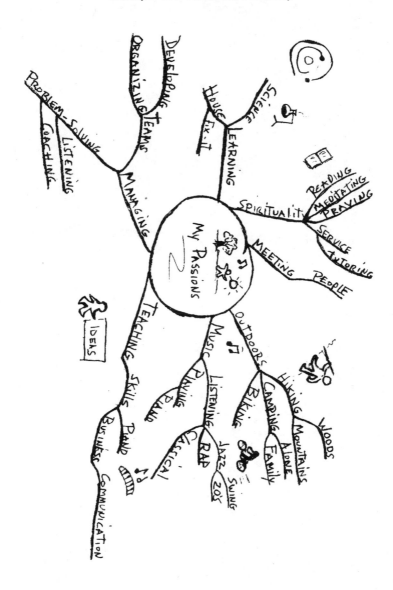

Worksheet: Your Passions Mindmap

In teaching this topic, I've often asked a room of 25 people to read aloud their top three or four passions. While there are certainly some repeated items, it is always amazing to hear the variety of passions—from sailing to building cabinets, playing on the beach to writing music, dancing to riding horses, collecting stamps to building teams.

It's even more revealing to find out the way people look at the same passions. Maybe half the people will have something dealing with the outdoors in their top passions, but for some it's about being in nature while for others it's about having an adventure, or feeling peaceful, or being challenged, or experiencing beauty. That's why we need to look more closely at the passions we've mapped and find out what are the driving elements of each passion, as we'll do in the next exercise.

EXERCISE 5: What I Love Most about My Passions

Purpose
❑ To determine what you most love about each passion
What You Need
❑ Mindmap example (What I Love Most about My Passions)
❑ Unlined paper or the Passions Mindmap Worksheet that follows the instructions
❑ Pens or markers in a variety of colors
❑ Your passions mindmap from Exercise 4
❑ 15–20 minutes
What To Do
1. When you are done with your mindmap, review your passions. Place the letter A next to the most important ones (as many as you'd like).
2. Next, take another piece of paper. Do a mindmap with the words *Passions: What I Love* or *What I Love Most About My Passions* in the center. Radiate out from that the A level passions you just labeled. Divide each branch into what you most love about each passion. Feel free to put any positive association, any keywords, that come to mind that capture

what you love about your passions. For example, one A level passion might be playing piano. You may love the creativity of playing, the sense of mastery, the beauty, the physicality. Each of those words—creativity, mastery, beauty, and physicality—would go on a different sub-branch.

3. Do the same with each of the other passions, using similar or different words as they come to you.

This exercise isn't about justifying your passion or saying *why* you like some activity, only *what you like about it*. For instance, to take a very simple example, you love eating vanilla ice cream simply because you love it, not for any involved set of reasons. But *what factors* you like about vanilla ice cream, a more specific definition of the parts you like can include—the taste, the sweetness, the color, the feeling on your tongue, the coolness, the memories it evokes. That's what you like. But it's not a justification.

Example of Passions Mindmap:
What I Love Most about My Passions

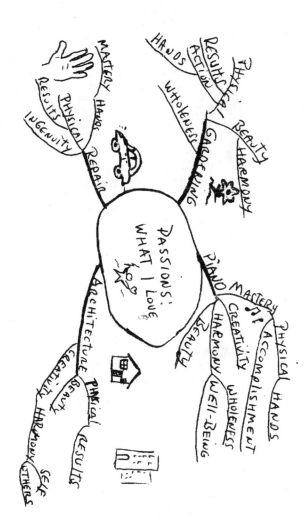

Passions Mindmap:
What I Love Most about My Passions

Let's see how this new mindmap adds to your understanding of yourself and your driving passions and interests.

I once demonstrated this exercise on the board using my passions as an example and in the process kept writing down the word creativity to describe what I most loved about many of the activities. The fact that I love being creative and helping others be creative was not news to me. The fact that it just kept popping up in relation to so many unrelated activities, however, led me to think again about how to make it more central to my workshops and writings. I recognized that it was so important it became part of a trademark phrase I used for my business ("bringing creativity to life").

Take another example (see the mindmap illustration on page 37). You may have said to yourself: "I've always known I love playing the piano, but I don't play at an advanced enough level to pursue it as a career. I can't do what I most want and have to find something else." But in doing this mindmap you may jot down revealing keywords and terms to capture what you love about playing the piano. The mindmap example shows a branch labeled mastery, further defined as a physical mastery using one's hands. There are also branches about having a feeling of harmony and well being, and experiencing beauty and one's creativity.

Another passion is gardening. Some of the keywords that come up in relation to that passion are the same as the ones you had for playing piano, such as hands, wholeness, physical action and results, well-being, harmony, and beauty. A pattern is developing that may extend to other activities you do and maybe to some you haven't tried yet. Using the mindmaps, you may realize that you want to work with your hands in creating something beautiful and in an activity that gives you a sense of wholeness and well being, perhaps even a sense of communing with something larger. In addition, while car repair doesn't include the words beauty or harmony, it does include the words hands and mastery and, like gardening, achieving physical results. Ingenuity appears which may or may not be similar to what you mean by creativity.

All these similarities mean that you no longer are limited to looking at gardening or music or car repair as lifework activities. You can now look for other activities that produce the same passion and satisfaction. Maybe you want to study architecture, cabinet making, sculpture, product design, or massage. Architecture is already listed on your mind map. Or you may find a new way into music or gardening that emphasizes some of the key elements you love but in ways that might help you create a career, such as helping others understand music so they can feel the sense of beauty and wholeness you experience.

So far you've worked with the main passions and with what you love about them. There is a third way to work with your passions—finding out which tasks you most love when doing each passionate activity. As an example, let's say you have a main branch of your original passions mindmap with the word camping on it. Ask yourself what tasks do you have to do in order to go camping. These tasks may include everything from planning the trip to setting up and taking down tents, from walking in the wild to cooking over a campfire. If you put down organizing work teams, think about the tasks needed to successfully organize a team—from choosing team members (evaluating qualifications) to shaping a common mission (envisioning), from motivating members to helping them resolve conflicts, from serving as a resource for them to serving as a link to the rest of the organization. The following exercise will give you the chance to mindmap the tasks behind each of your major passions.

EXERCISE 6: Tasks Mindmap

Purpose
- ☐ To determine the specific tasks you most love
- ☐ To see how you might transfer these tasks to new fields of activity and to your lifework vision

What you need

❑ Unlined paper or the mindmap worksheet on page 42 and the list worksheet on page 43

❑ Pens and colored markers

❑ 15–20 minutes

What To Do

1. Again place on a mindmap your key passions. This time note all the component tasks for performing or doing that passion. These tasks can be noted as action verbs with "ing" endings, such as planning, reading, or exercising. The same task may show up a number of times next to different main passions.

2. Place an A next to all tasks you enjoy, a B next to those you are neutral about or only enjoy sometimes, and a C next to those you don't enjoy.

3. List the A tasks on a separate worksheet and note how many times each of those tasks were noted on the mindmap.

Passions Mindmap: Tasks I Love Doing

Worksheet: List of "A" Level Tasks

1.

2.

3.

4.

5.

6.

7.

8.

9.

10.

Let's see how this list of tasks might give you new insight into what you want to do. What if you listed as a passion, family vacations. Not surprisingly, you dismissed that passion as irrelevant to your lifework search because you are concerned with a more satisfying career and don't see how anyone will pay you to go on a family vacation. (Of course, it's not as ridiculous as it sounds because some people do get paid for going on vacations, including travel writers and photographers). On your tasks mindmap, though, you see that next to family vacations you have branches that show such tasks as researching (finding out interesting and appropriate places for your trip), consulting (with family members about their preferences), organizing (the itinerary), packing, and resolving disagreements. Some of those tasks you like and others not. The ones you like are elements of what you might want in your job. They might also reveal what kind of job descriptions to pursue since each of those tasks you love involves a corresponding skill that organizations need.

Better yet, you may find certain kinds of tasks repeating as you review your different passions. For instance, you may list among your passions—doing crossword puzzles, repairing cars, and talking with friends about personal issues. These seem unrelated and, except for the car repair, not much to do with determining a career that will pay you money (assuming that is your goal). But maybe for you, all of these passions involve researching for clues and using them to solve a mystery. In other words, they are all about detective work. That's obvious in doing puzzles, but it also can apply to what you most love about fixing cars—figuring out what's wrong and how to fix the problems. Maybe performing the actual repair work is secondary. When talking with friends you may like best helping them figure out what their problems are by looking at all the evidence. If that's the case you probably would need to include a clue-gathering, researching, analyzing, problem-solving kind of career, even if it has nothing to do with cars, friends, and puzzles.

Review all three mindmaps—key passions, key qualities of the passions you love, key tasks you love. Put them together and you have a potent list of the kinds of things you will need for your lifework. Not everything will fit in with your central purpose, but playing with combinations of these three key areas will help you generate new possibilities.

EXERCISE 7: Passions and People

Purpose:
- [ ] To get new ideas to help you
- [ ] To feel how much support is available
- [ ] To hear yourself talk about what was previously only in your head or on paper. Often that can make a remarkable difference. Participants in my lifework classes often begin feeling a little sheepish about admitting their passions but end up recognizing how creative and unique they are.

What You Need:
- [ ] Your passions mindmaps and related lists
- [ ] One or more friends/relatives who are willing to help
- [ ] Key Ideas Worksheet
- [ ] Pen or pencil
- [ ] 15–30 minutes with each person or group

What To Do
1. Make it a game. One at a time or in groups of two or three, bring in family members or friends you trust and show them your mindmaps.
2. Talk them through your thinking about each passion, what you love about it and about your favorite tasks, using the mindmaps as an illustration when helpful.
3. Ask the person or group to mirror back *exactly* what you said so *you* can hear it. It's a completely different experience hearing someone else say what you were thinking and saying or thinking it yourself. Different senses and thought processes are involved. You have more distance to reflect on what you are thinking as well. In the communication classes I lead, mirroring is the first technique I always teach where one person simply repeats back what another has said. It assures the speaker that the listener has accurately heard what was said, gives the speaker a sense of completion simply from being heard, and often gives the speaker enough distance to better understand what he or she just said.

4. Ask them if there is any passion you have left out that they have seen you express at some time. Ask them if there is any pattern they notice that might open up your thinking.

5. On the following worksheet, jot down any ideas you have heard or had on your own that you want to explore or remember. Refer back to them and your mindmaps as you work on later exercises about what you want to do (especially in devising your core and lifework summary statements in chapter 5) and where you want to do it.

A note of caution: Choose people who will be supportive and who you trust. Remember that no matter how wise or helpful they are, only you can determine your vision and goals. Others can definitely help you find your path, but you have to decide on what is best for you with their guidance, not with their demands or expectations.

Most people find these exercises exciting and revealing, and some learn things beyond the realm of career and calling. A lifework student I'll call Sara completed her passions mindmap in class. Sara was excited about seeing in front of her the primary passions of her life and how they connected. She used it to talk with her boyfriend about her dreams and hopes. As she did so she recognized that her relationship with her boyfriend Tom was compatible with or central to her other passions. She also realized that having a child, which Tom didn't want to do and Sara did, had been holding up their possible engagement. Yet when she drew her mindmap, having children was nowhere to be found. Even when she thought of including it, it didn't seem to be a central branch. This led her to examine her heart more closely and realize she was ready to marry Tom.

Another student was looking for ways to incorporate his love of the outdoors into a new career and came to appreciate how deeply he felt about his upbringing in New Zealand, especially time with his grandmother. That insight itself was important. In addition, he began to see ways he might teach about the outdoors, incorporating his grandmother's native wisdom.

**Worksheet: Key Ideas and Notes from Passions Exercises
and Mindmaps**

Chapter 4. Integrity and Values

You now have more clearly identified your passions and what ties them together. You know about putting attention on universal gifts and knowing your particular talents and skills. You are now ready to see how to put them together into a mission or purpose. But you also need to answer a different kind of *who am I* question, not so much about what skills you have or what passions, but the principles you use in deciding how to act and, in some cases, what you will and won't do. These are your values.

You'll use mindmapping again as a start and then find out how you can actively work with your values to be more dynamic and effective, while being true to yourself.

EXERCISE 8: Prioritizing Your Values

Purpose
❑ To clarify and affirm to yourself what your key values are and how they relate to each other

What You Need
❑ The Values Mindmap and Top 10 Values Worksheets that follow the instructions
❑ Pens and colored markers
❑ 20–30 minutes

What To Do

1. Mindmap your values, using an image to represent your values and single words on branches to represent each value. Use the list that follows, which comes from values people have often used in my workshops, to stimulate your own thinking.

EXAMPLES OF VALUES

Acceptance	Achievement	Adventure
Community	Creativity	Diversity
Faith	Family	Friendship
Growth	Honesty	Humor
Independence	Intimacy	Learning
Love	Loyalty	Newness
Nonattachment	Peace	Play
Respect	Risk	Serenity
Service	Tradition	Trust

2. Once you've completed your mindmap, including images to represent or express individual values, rank the top ten values, placing a small number 1, 2, 3, etc. next to the appropriate value.

3. In a journal or in discussion with someone you trust, explain your thinking about the values and their order, focusing especially on your top value. Discuss how it applies to your life. You aren't justifying or defending your list or asking someone to challenge you about your values or how they play out in your life. You are noticing your own thinking on this subject.

4. List the top 10 values in order on a separate piece of paper or in this book on page 52.

5. Put down any final notes you have now that you've written about or talked about your values list, anything you noticed. For instance, workshop participants have often said how they saw how everything flowed out of their top value. They

might say that without the value of honesty, nothing else can be trusted. Or without faith, life would be purposeless.

6. As a more extensive follow-up exercise, go through a 24-hour period consciously doing your best to live according to your top value. Don't contradict other values, but focus on the top one. Check in with yourself about your actions throughout the day to see how your value does or could shape your behavior and how it affects those around you. At the end of the day, journal about what you noticed.

Worksheet: Values Mindmap

Worksheet: Top 10 Values in Order

1.

2.

3.

4.

5.

6.

7.

8.

9.

10.

Most people feel happy or comforted reviewing their values. That's wonderful. Acknowledging our values should bring a sense of peace or happiness, even as they may challenge us to do better in our lives. Most of us are also very identified with our values. They seem fundamental to our personalities and identities. We may think: "Without having honesty (or compassion or faith or love) as a top value, I wouldn't be able to be me."

But as important as our values are, they are not us. We are more than our values. We have chosen them. We can re-chose them, if we so desire.

EXERCISE 9: Re-evaluating Your Values

Purpose
❑ To act in new, positive ways and re-evaluate what is possible or desirable
What You Need
❑ Your Top 10 Values Worksheet from the previous exercise
❑ The two worksheets that follow

❑ Pen or pencil
❑ Your imagination and room to move
❑ 15–20 minutes for the basic exercise

What To Do

1. Review your list of 10 values. Make a second list, placing the tenth or ninth value as a top value, and placing your original top value on the bottom of the list. See if you now want to change the order of any of the other values. Now review the new list.

2. Close your eyes and imagine how you would have gone through the last 24 hours if you had lived your life with that new value as your top priority.

3. Jot down any ideas or feelings that arise, including any negative feelings.

4. Stand up and for the next five minutes, walk, talk, and observe what is around you in your new identity. If confidence is now tops, act as if you are supremely confident, if beauty, then take time to notice and express beauty, if honesty, note how authentic your motives or thoughts are.

5. As a more extensive follow-up exercise, using the same value, or choosing another one, go through a 24-hour period consciously acting as if this is your top value and of utmost importance to you. Try a different value another day.

Note what effect this has on your life. I've had people in my classes tell me they completely re-envisioned their lives by simply putting creativity first instead of last or emphasizing adventure instead of peace. It's as if there is a room in your house that you know exists but have never entered; now that you've entered it, you have found new things you can do while in that room that you couldn't or didn't do before. Class members who feel this way often come back to the next session with exciting stories about meeting new people and taking new risks on their jobs that led them to see themselves differently.

After your experiment, you can decide what, if anything, you want to do about your values. You can decide to creatively shift them around, or you might want to focus on a particular value just as you might on a particular friendship or activity just for a day, week, or month in order to strengthen that value in your life. Or you might feel your original list is what makes the most sense to you. No matter what you decide, take responsibility for where your values are leading you, and know that you are larger than your values.

Worksheet: Top 10 Values Re-Prioritized

1.

2.

3.

4.

5.

6.

7.

8.

9.

10.

Worksheet: Notes on Re-prioritizing Values

Putting It Together, Moving Ahead

You have now recognized where you have succeeded and how this relates to universal gifts of compassion, energy, etc. You have looked at your unique gifts and skills in the context of your varied intelligences. You have clarified your values and taken a bold and creative look at how you can work with them while remaining in integrity with yourself and your beliefs. And you have seen the emotional drive behind everything in terms of your passions, the engine of change.

Most likely you have had a few *aha* experiences that clarified for you what is most important in your work and public life. Perhaps you have felt affirmed in what you already knew and now feel more ready to move ahead. In any case, what you have done is to tease out the elements of your lifework that will form the basis of the jobs or activities you will do to create a sense of fulfillment, joy, and meaning.

While you can certainly ponder your answers for a long time (and redoing these exercises is recommended on a regular basis), you are ready to move on to the second of our four questions. You now have a clearer idea of who you are and now have to see what you want to do.

Before moving on, take a moment to review your three or four original goals you wrote down at the start of this book. Are you beginning to accomplish them? Do they still seem relevant or do they need modifying? Make sure you are on track with your goals as you go through this process.

WHAT IS MY PURPOSE?

Chapter 5. Your Primary Mission

"So, what do you do?" When you first meet someone, how often have you asked or been asked that question? In our society, that question usually means, what is your line of work. For those with clear-cut titles or job descriptions—I manage a branch of a bank, I do hair styling, I package software, I teach economics, I sell life insurance—the answer can be brief and easy.

For others, especially those in consulting, it can be more complex—I consult with clients about leadership development and organizational efficiency (which can mean anything from facilitation training to seminars on downsizing). Even if you can employ a simple and quick description, it doesn't often get to the heart of what you do. You may sell life insurance, but what does that really mean to you? If you understand and work from a deeper level, you know you are really providing protection and psychological comfort while reducing financial risk. You are also an advisor if you are doing your job right. That doesn't always come across in the message, "I sell life insurance."

For all of us, it's useful to take stock and determine what is our real purpose at work, even if we are fine with our current work, such as our hypothetical life insurance salesperson. Determining our purpose or mission is much like what a business organization needs to do. Some businesses do this very well with a great deal of staff input, while others put up ignored mission statements on the walls that make generic statements. (The mission of XYZ Company is to produce the best product possible for our customers while offering the most wholesome and successful work environment for our employees.) You'll want to do something that you are inspired by, not something that will hang on your wall as ignored decoration. We'll call your personal mission statement a *lifework summary statement* (LSS).

Your LSS tells in a sentence or two what really matters about your job. As with the life insurance salesperson you want it to describe the underlying purpose of your work, what you are working to accomplish. Eventually, you might use it to develop a public statement that may be the basis of marketing yourself or your business, but for now you want to develop a statement that works for you, whether or not it is something you want others to see and hear.

The LSS will assist you in two key ways. First, it will lead you into a creative process that will help you clarify your thinking. The final statement is important, but having gone through the process of fashioning the statement will connect you with your vision and remove all the fuzzy options, maybes, and sort-ofs that tend to fill our minds when we haven't defined something.

Second, once it's developed, your LSS serves as a mental rudder to keep you on course. You'll be able to see if what you are planning is consistent with your LSS. For instance, you may hold a job that satisfies your LSS and then have an opportunity for promotion which seems exciting but actually will lead you away from your lifework goals. This often happens to people who start businesses with new creative ideas and wind up spending their time in management which they dislike. For instance, one person started a scientific testing company. He loved the actual scientific elements of his job, but he was so successful that he wound up having to hire a significant number of employees and spent his time managing them and the business. He succeeded but had lost track of his deeper mission. Eventually, he and his partner sold the business and started a new company where they both could recapture the roles they really loved.

Similarly, I am often asked to provide training that's related to what I do but different from what I have been doing. That can be great. It can expand my own thinking and move me in appropriate new directions. Or, it can lead me to something I can do but is not what I want to do.

Developing an LSS may sound difficult, but it can be an inventive activity that is enjoyable and helpful if you exploit the playful side of your personality. The exercise below will take you through a proven process that will allow many ideas and discoveries come to you if you are willing to let them. As you'll see, the exercise isn't built on finding the one true statement immediately. It also incorporates humor to help you loosen up and think in new directions.

Your statement will be short, focused, and built upon everything you've just completed in answering the *who am I* question. In other words, you will be taking your passions and values and gifts and saying how you will apply them to everyday life.

Examples of lifework summary statements:

- I organize groups to take direct actions to save our natural environment.
- I counsel couples so they can create the loving relationships they most want.
- I develop software programs that allow people to pull together information more effectively and creatively with minimum need of technical skills.
- I help people work together more harmoniously and productively in a business environment through conflict resolution training.
- I show people how to make their dream of owning a home become a reality by helping them in the mortgage process.

That kind of statement can seem too difficult at first. It's often best to start with a more basic statement, a **core statement**.

A core statement is a simple sentence that expresses what you most love to do or be and can't live without. It is about your core personality and is based on your key passions.

Here are some examples of core statements. You'll see how simple and direct they are:

- I love being around children.
- I love being in nature.
- I love working with my hands.
- I love being funny.
- I love teaching.
- I love gardening.
- I love writing and speaking.
- I love helping people solve problems.
- I love playing with numbers.
- I love being creative with physical objects.
- I love learning.
- I love adventure.
- I love exploring new cultures.
- I love harmony and peace.
- I love beautiful objects.
- I love testing out ideas scientifically.

EXERCISE 10: Writing Your Core Statement

Purpose
❑ To summarize your core passions and values
What You Need
❑ Core Statements Worksheet that follows the instructions
❑ Pen or pencil
❑ Your passions mindmaps from chapter 3
❑ 15 minutes
What To Do
1. Return to your passion mindmaps. Review your key passions as well as what you love about them and your key tasks and write about 10 core statements. What often stops people

here is trying to choose, picking the best passion or the true core statement. That's like trying to be creative and simultaneously searching for the one best answer. Those are two different activities. First generate lots of answers. Then you can see what you have. "The best way to have good ideas is to have lots of ideas," as two-time Nobel Laureate Linus Pauling said.

2. Get goofy. To help you generate lots of ideas and to have more fun with all this "serious" work, include at least three silly core statements that are the exact opposite of what you really love. For instance, if your core statement is, "I love walking in nature in quiet, open settings," then an opposite silly statement could be: "I love walking along highways where I am forced to breathe unhealthy fumes and can barely hear myself think." The more detailed and opposite, the better. Participants in my classes not only start laughing while writing these, but often find unexpected insights as they see that the opposites may include some truth (I love being with lots of people doing team activities vs. I love being alone and reflecting on things. You may find that the second is a real, but neglected part of your life.)

3. Add to your list if you think of something you left out. Eliminate those that you don't really love (but don't eliminate those that you love but haven't been doing or those that seem hard to do).

4. Star all statements that are vital and important to you.

5. See if you can combine any of the statements. For example: I love being around children; I love being funny; I love helping others though teaching; and I love expressing my creativity through writing and speaking might all be combined into: I love teaching children how to be more creative. Don't be concerned if attempts at combining seem awkward at first. Just get into the process and trust that you can develop and improve your statements over time.

Worksheet: Core Statements

1.

2.

3.

4.

5.

6.

7.

8.

9.

10.

EXERCISE 11: Writing Your Lifework Summary Statement

Purpose

❑ To put into a simple sentence or two the main direction of your lifework

What You Need

❑ Your list of core statements
❑ Lifework Summary Statement Worksheet
❑ Pen or pencil
❑ 30–45 minutes

What To Do

Now you have before you a few compact statements about what you love. Your next task is to turn each one into a potential lifework summary statement. Remember that these statements transform your core statements from what you are passionate about into how you bring that passion into the world.

1. Review the following list of core statements and their corresponding lifework summary statements.

Core: I love to foster harmony between people.
LSS: I counsel couples so that they can create the loving relationships they most want.
Or
LSS: I help people work together more harmoniously and productively in a business environment through conflict resolution training.

Core: I love helping young children grow and explore their world.
LSS: I create toys and games for children so they are challenged to think and grow.
Or
LSS: I teach children about the wonders of the natural world in a museum setting.

Core: I love reading mysteries and trying to puzzle out their intricacies.

LSS: I manage a mystery bookstore where I help people find just the right kinds of mysteries and lead discussion groups in the evening.

Or

LSS: I edit books for a publisher specializing in mysteries.

2. Choose one of your core statements and imagine what you might do to express that core passion.

3. Write a number of possible lifework summary statements that might relate to that core statement. Even if they don't quite suit you, it will get you thinking expansively about possibilities instead of narrowly about the right or wrong statement. You may want to start with a few opposite, silly statements. One class participant wrote as an opposite mission: I work at a repetitive task all day in a windowless cubicle with no real purpose. It was an opposite statement, but it startled her because as she put it, "That perfectly describes what I do now."

4. Write a LSS for your other core statements.

5. If you feel stuck, it often helps to just start writing without a lot of editing and forethought. Instead of working hard at these statements, just give yourself a one-minute time limit and write whatever comes to mind on the topic of your core statement. Do this a few times and you'll probably have the makings of a practical statement.

6. Review your statements and see if there are two or three that apply to you and might serve as guides for you.

7. Keep playing with your favorite statements—editing, tweaking, showing it to others for ideas (not for their approval necessarily), and generally massaging it into something that makes you feel great when you read it. It doesn't need to be absolutely clear to others, but it needs to be very clear and satisfying to you.

8. Recognize you can change or alter it any time, but that it will temporarily guide you and keep you on course with your lifework journey.

This is an ongoing task. Every few months I review my LSS and play with it. Sometimes I wind up making no changes. Other times I realize more clearly what is essential to me and alter the statement. I also refer back to my LSS to help decide if new projects are a good match.

Worksheet: My Lifework Summary Statements (LSS)

1.

2.

3.

4.

Chapter 6. Add to Your Experience: Use Someone Else's

Maybe you're not ready to write your lifework summary statement (LSS) even though you have successfully completed the exercises in the *who am I* chapters. People of all ages, but especially those who have had less experience in the workforce, or people coming to this country from a significantly different culture may not be aware of all of the jobs they can do or all of the work roles they can perform. I have found that teaching lifework to high school students, for example, was not very helpful until the students began to investigate what kinds of occupations existed, what skills the occupations required, and what tasks they would have to do to fill those positions. While I don't believe in limiting people to set occupational roles that already exist and are nicely coded for your 1040 tax form, I do believe people need to have a wide sampling of possibilities before they can choose or even create a new kind of position for themselves.

If you are stuck because you aren't sure what kinds of things you can do with your skills and talents, it would probably be helpful to take a trip to the library or onto the internet and locate the many books and resources that describe various kinds of jobs and careers.

As you narrow down your interests, informational interviews with people in your chosen field become extremely valuable. They can offer you the inside scoop about what you really would spend each day doing. A glamorous title doesn't promise glamorous activities.

Most people are very willing to provide informational interviews as long as you respect them and their time. That simply means you set a time at their convenience, with a time limit they agree to, and then stick to it. You need to have a set of questions in mind to get the answers you need and, equally important, to make sure the other person doesn't wander off into favorite stories about coworkers or other irrelevant information.

Who should you call? Anyone in a potentially interesting field, whether you know the person or were referenced to that person by a friend, colleague, family member, previous informational interview contact, or anyone else on your networking list of resources (see chapter 9 on networking).

Informational interviews can often be the fastest and most practical way to get the information you need about a variety of topics—from what a certain job or company is like to what educational path is best for your needs. But if you go into an interview unprepared, you may find you have wasted your time and the time of the person you are interviewing. Here are a few tips for succeeding at such interviews.

Informational Interview Tips

1. *Know your goal.* Determine in advance what the key information is that you want. For instance, you don't need to hear how a person got to where he or she is if your focus is on how independent that person can be when performing that job.

2. *Prepare questions.* (Sample questions are provided below in the next section.) Bring them with you—not to read one after another, but to make sure you don't forget anything. You may want to take notes during the interview, unless that will keep you from staying engaged and making good eye contact.

3. *Relax. Be yourself.* Even though you have a clear focus and goal, think of the interview as a conversation rather than as a chance to pick someone's brain.

4. *Stick to the topic.* Begin by telling or reminding the person who you are and why you're doing the interview.

5. *Ask for advice where appropriate.* Even if you don't like people telling you what to do, ask for advice around your key point. That is often a great way to get someone to tell you what they really think about something.

6. *Stick to the time limits.* If you are running over, *you* need to make the point that the agreed-upon time is up and you don't want to take up any more of the person's time. If you both have more time and want to talk more, go ahead. But make it the other person's option.

7. *Give thanks.* No matter how the interview went, always thank the person and always send a thank-you note. Send it within 24 hours if at all possible. You can have a simple template or form note, but whenever possible include a few specifics about how the talk helped you (such as, "the information about training programs will help me take another step toward my goal of becoming a world class juggler"). A personal handwritten note on a thank-you card is particularly nice, but a simple email will also do in almost all cases. A thank-you note is not only thoughtful. It shows you are professional and will make it easier to contact the person again if you ever need to for any reason.

Sample Informational Interview Questions

Below is a set of starter questions to help you formulate your own interview questions. The key is to remember why you are talking to this person in the first place. Is it to understand how to have the same kind of job that person has, or to learn what the daily work schedule is like, or to find out how many hours per week is typical in a particular job? Not every informational interview should go after the same information.

Questions about the Job

1. What are your main responsibilities? Which most interest you?

2. What level person do you report to? What is their position? How do you and that person connect with the rest of the organization?

3. How do you spend most of your time at work? What are the main tasks and what skills do they involve (such as communication skills, computer skills, etc.)

4. What do you like most about your work? Why?

5. If you could change anything you wanted to at work, what would you change and why?

Questions about Their Career Paths

6. How did you decide to do the work you are doing?

7. What kind of education/training did you have?

8. What part of your education/training has proven most useful to you in your work life?

9. What other jobs have you had? How did each help you get to where you are today? How did you get this particular job?

10. Looking back, would you have made some different choices to get to where you are today? If so, what would they be?

11. What career/work plans do you have for the future?

Asking for Advice

12. Examples: I'm planning for a career in___. What advice would you have for me? Or, I haven't decided yet what I want to do next in my career. What advice do you have that might help me decide?

WHERE DO I WORK?

Chapter 7. Picture This

We always hear about getting the big picture. That's what your lifework summary statement (LSS) is about. The big picture lets you know you are managing a toy company, teaching parasailing, coaching kids, or helping others resolve problems. But when you form an image of that lifework, what does it look like? If someone followed you around for a day what might she observe? Specifically, where is this action occurring? With whom? When and how often? In short, the where question is really a series of questions that get at *what it looks like* when you are working within that big picture.

You will be answering that series of where questions by imagining and recording a mental picture of this wonderful scene from your daily work life. And it's easy. All you'll have to do is daydream and report on what you dreamt.

Daydreaming can be one of the most rewarding and refreshing activities of our day, though it has come to mean wasting time. Don't worry about wasting time in this case. You will be putting your time to good use answering all the where-related questions by daydreaming what it would be like to live your ideal life, or rather, a single, typical (not necessarily perfect) day in your ideal life.

Sometimes lifework class members groan at this point and tell me that if they knew those details they wouldn't be in the class. They'd be doing what they most love. My answer: relax.

You'll find more answers than you thought if you relax. Relaxation is the key to daydreaming. You are just playing here, not coming up with the right answer on a test, not giving a final answer for a million dollars on TV. You are dreaming up possibilities based on what you do know so far, like an artist photographing scenes until finding the one that works just right or a poet trying out lines on the page to know what is possible, or even a scientist testing a hypothesis. You might want to come up with a few different scenarios and play through each, testing how good and energized or tired and anxious they make you feel. The next exercise will give you some tips on how to do and record this daydreaming.

In my classes and coaching, I've watched people really light up talking about their day in the ideal life. Some proved irresistible not only to the creator but also to everyone else in the class.

One woman had written about an ideal day managing a retreat center. Just a week earlier the center was only one vague idea among many. After presenting it to her small group, they began chiming in how they'd like to go there and had a wealth of ideas for how to make it successful—from fireplaces to meditation rooms. Soon, the entire class was drawn into the discussion because her vision and energy was so clear and powerful and authentic. If her center was up and running at that moment she would have had a class full of eager customers.

EXERCISE 12: Twenty-Four Hours in Your Ideal Life: A Day Log

Purpose
- ❏ To generate the details of your lifework vision
- ❏ To connect with feelings of satisfaction and put an image to them
- ❏ To determine what it looks like when you are doing what you love to do

What You Need
- ❑ A relaxing space
- ❑ Day Log Worksheet
- ❑ Pen or pencil
- ❑ A willingness to dream big
- ❑ 30 minutes when you're not feeling crunched

What To Do

1. Do whatever works for you to get centered and relaxed. You don't want to be sleepy but you certainly want to feel at ease and comfortable. Don't try to squeeze this exercise in between other time-pressured tasks or while multi-tasking or while your six-year-old will be constantly tugging at your arm. For some, it's best to sit alone in a quiet space at home. For others, a walk in the woods might be best. You just want to be at ease, clearheaded, and focused on the task.

2. Imagine a day in your life as if it was one of many as you live your ideal life. It doesn't need to be an ideal day, but a *typical work day if you had all the elements of your life the way you most would like them to be.*

3. Specifically, start with when you wake up. Is it early to enjoy a sunrise, or are you waking up whenever you do because you want to sleep in? Where do you wake up? In New York City? In Sri Lanka? What's around you? Do you see the Hawaiian surf or the Statue of Liberty out your window? A forest? Your sister's house across the street? Are you in a large house or a cabin or apartment? Is your spouse by your side? Are you alone? This is less about answering the questions and more about observing what comes most easily and happily to mind.

4. Write down what you are imagining as a detailed day's log. Put in the times to help track your actions. Include all your significant activities from waking up to going to sleep. When do you start work? Do you do it in a home office? Do you bike to work? Take a bus? Get chauffeured? Walk along a nature trail? When you arrive, what time is it? What tasks do

you start doing? Who's there to help you? What challenges are you facing this particular day?

5. If you aren't sure what you'd do, review your LSS or passions mind map and just try out a scene as if you are putting together a little piece of fiction that suits your own interests.

When you have completed your day's log, put it away for a day or two and then reread it. Does it still appeal to you? Do you want to add or subtract something? Do you feel you'd like to try a different scenario? By all means write up a completely different day. Or you may feel as many of my students do that the one day wasn't long enough to get in all their favorite activities. They often write up additional days based on the same larger vision. That's great to do as well.

Worksheet: My Day Log

Day Log continued:

When you've put together enough daily logs to feel you've covered all the basics, notice how you've answered the questions of where, with whom, when, what does it look like.

Now you are ready for the Magic Wand Test.

EXERCISE 13: Magic Wand Test

Purpose
☐ To get a gut, intuitive response to your daydream
☐ To find some of the hidden doubts, anxieties, and un-claimed hopes

What You Need
☐ A friend
☐ A magic wand (really!) of your choice. (Glittery pencils or favorite sticks can sometimes be magical.)
☐ Your day log exercise
☐ 10–15 minutes

What To Do
1. Ask your friend to listen closely as you summarize your day as you described it in your day log, or read it aloud.
2. Ask your friend to mirror back to you all the key elements he or she heard. This should be done with some detail, and not an offhanded general summary. In other words, "I heard you talk about getting up with the sun so you could spend a half hour outside walking in the fresh air," vs. a summary that merely says, "You get up early and walk outside." The second doesn't capture the details or the spirit of your entry, and that's crucial for the magic wand test.
3. You need to listen closely to your friend's rendition of your day. As we saw earlier, hearing someone else summarize or mirror it is very different from speaking and daydreaming it. Often it reveals how much you really want something or how something may be missing or not quite right. In this step, notice how you are reacting to the different elements of your own story. Feel free to tell your friend of any

changes you'd now like to make and have the friend mirror those changes back to you for retesting.

4. Once you have completed this process and have heard all the details without feeling a need for change, you're ready to take the magic wand test: Your friend should lift up the wand, wave it generously over your head and say boldly: "Your wish has been granted. There's no turning back. From this moment on, you are living exactly the life you have dreamed." In other words, everything you just described is now true for you—the rising with the sun for a walk in Hawaii and working with cooperative and brilliant colleagues overlooking the water, solving problems about transportation in cities (or whatever your daydream was). The question for you is this: Now that it's real and you actually have to live this life, how do you feel? Does it feel like everything you had hoped? Or does it make your stomach queasy? Is there one more thing that's been missing you'd like to add?

5. Answer the question from a gut level. Often I find people say yes, that's it...except...and then they say what's missing that they haven't been fully aware of or didn't dare to put in their ideal day log. The magic wand test is usually pretty magical, pulling out the deeper truths from everyone who tries it.

6. If you find there's something you need to add or change after the magic wand test, feel free to request it from your friend who will then say something like, "OK. We will now wave the wand and change your life to include (whatever you just wanted to change)." Now see how you feel. Do this up to three or four times. After that, the magic does seem to start wearing off.

This is a particularly good exercise to share back and forth. If you have a friend who is also going through this lifework process or else has some dreams of her own to clarify, then take turns waving the magic wand. When I first did this with a friend who has been my ongoing success partner, he felt happy and all set to go, except...he hadn't included any travel in his work life so we added that. Then he was happy except...he wasn't sure he had enough time for his family life so we altered that and he was happy except.... We did this a few times until the gut feeling he had was solid and content. When you get that queasy feeling like you just swallowed a bug, something isn't right yet. Look inside and identify what it's about.

It can be a dream you haven't admitted or something you don't quite want to do, or it can be just self-doubt and anxiety. Some people have come up with what they'd love but because they don't believe they can have it, they say they're not sure they want it. Or they may want it and believe it could happen, but are afraid they may fail at whatever they are hoping to do. Such doubts and fears are perfectly fine, so long as you can identify them for what they are (namely, fears and anxieties and doubts) and not be stopped by them or mislabel them as proof that the dream isn't quite right. Once they are identified as doubts and you allow them to be there, they will usually ease up, and you will know you may need to confront them directly. But this should not stop you from marching forward with your dream.

When I tell groups that they can have fears, doubts, and questions *and* still go right ahead—that fears and action can exist simultaneously—some people are astonished as well as relieved. Suddenly there is no reason not to move ahead. You don't have to become perfect, fearless, without self-doubt, or have supreme self-confidence and self-esteem to move on and make your dream start coming true.

That doesn't mean you should avoid these issues. It only means that they don't have to stop you. Often, people create unnecessary blocks to their lifework process. I can't do what I love until I get over a fear, or until my kids are grown, or until I have more money saved. After looking at the situation squarely and fully, people usually find those reasons to stop action are not valid.

You can take positive steps even as you work on the fear or nurture your kids or earn more money at a job you don't much like. And working on the fears, nurturing the kids, and making money can all be part of your vision and your plan, rather than side problems that distract you.

It's true that if you can reduce the fear or anxiety, you may find it easier to move ahead. And that's very good to do, of course. It's also true that moving ahead can also help reduce the fear or anxiety or doubt. It works both ways.

HOW DO I SUCCEED?

Chapter 8. Action Plans

By now you've at least begun the process of answering *Who*, *What*, and *Where*, and now it's time to answer the *How* question—How can I make my vision come true? How can I make it real? (How can I bring out who I am by doing what I do where and when I want to do it?) Answering this question brings out your inner quest into the larger world. It's about acting step by step, and sometimes leap by hopeful leap, to realize your vision.

Taking the Middle Road

There's a spectrum of responses to planning. For some, planning is about as palatable as getting a root canal while recovering from the flu. For others, there's nothing more satisfying than filling out a day timer or organizing a to-do list for themselves, their colleagues, their families, and their neighbor's cat.

For the first group, please realize that a plan is like a map. Without a map for a long trip to unknown territories, you can certainly have great adventures but may not get to where you're going or get there much later than you would like. Is it necessary? Only if you want to increase your chances of succeeding in your vision. So it may be worth spending a little time now and then to keep updating the map and checking in with it. And for the people who plan even in their sleep, please realize a map won't help you if you don't actually take the journey. The map is a means to the end, not the goal itself unless your lifework is mapmaking. Don't spend half your time planning. Once you have answered the who, what, where questions it's time to get a basic map and start acting.

That means for all groups, you don't need to spend hours per week on planning. Instead, you need to spend enough time to have clear directions, but not so much that you map out actions for the distant future that will almost definitely change by the time you get there.

With this middle road of planning in mind, let's examine the basic way we're going to create action plans. Although it's great to have everything laid out in exquisite detail for the next months and years, all most of us need is a general overview for the major long-term steps we must take to reach our goal, and a more detailed look at what we need to do now—today, this week, this month, and next. After all, you can only act now. You can't do anything tomorrow until it becomes now.

You also want some freedom in your plan. Not only do things change over time, but you want to leave some breathing space in your plan to allow for unexpected opportunities and serendipitous connections. As soon as you set up a clear goal or vision, and commit to working on it, all kinds of unexpected things start to happen. You need to be prepared to act by knowing what you want (namely, your vision) and being ready to act when something new to get you there appears.

My lifework course participants come in excited by about the second or third week of class. They are eager to share with each other how a simple clarification of a goal led to meeting just the right person or to finding out about unexpected opportunities right under their noses. I hear stories all the time about wanting to work abroad and meeting at a party, someone in that field in Ireland or Poland or Thailand. One woman had finished the class while still in graduate school and knew just what she wanted but continued to believe she couldn't ask for so much. She was in public health and wanted opportunities to work in education with children in very particular ways. She had given up her goals until her adviser called her in to ask if she wanted to apply for a grant that had just come across her desk. The grant was to do exactly what the student had dreamed of doing. She didn't even have to seek out such a grant. The opportunity just landed in her lap.

Retirees who have no idea what to do with their free time suddenly find someone coming to them needing the kind of help their years of experience can provide (and in one case receiving his first bouquet of roses ever as a thank you).

I've heard so many stories like this that I now believe a clear goal and intention and continuing to take what steps we can toward that goal in a committed manner will produce far more than we can anticipate (thus the need to stay open for surprises over time). As Goethe wrote:

Until one is committed, there is hesitating, the chance to draw back, always ineffectiveness. Concerning all acts of initiative (and creation), there is one elementary truth, the ignorance of which kills countless ideas and splendid plans: that the moment one definitely commits oneself, the Providence moves too. All sorts of things occur to help one, that would never otherwise have occurred. A whole stream of events issue from the decision raising in one's favor all manner of unforeseen incidents and meetings and material assistance which no man could have dreamed would have come his way.

Drawing Up Your Action Plan

One way to take into account the future and use it to guide the present in much greater detail is to work backwards from your goal. Innovative thinkers from Edward de Bono, the internationally famed creativity guru to Barbara Sher, author of the groundbreaking career book, *Wishcraft*, talk about developing action plans backwards. Here's how to do it:

Look at your final goal and ask if you can simply accomplish your goal today. If not, what would have to be the final step that would get you there. If becoming a Broadway lead actor is your goal, right before you landed your first lead Broadway part, you might have auditioned for it. Can you do that now? No. OK, so what might come right before that? Perhaps you might have sent in a résumé or tape or made the right contacts. Are you ready to do any of those things today? No. OK, so what might come before that? Perform lead and supporting roles in significant productions Off or Off-Off Broadway or in regional theaters, perhaps. Are you ready to do that today? No? OK, so what might come before that?

And you keep on searching with your vision as guide until you find what you *can* do today. That sequence of events which gives you some action to do right now at one end and your goal at the other is your action plan, or at least the outline for your plan.

Once you determine the major sequence of actions, it's time to list them on a timeline (see Exercise 14 and the timeline examples following the exercise). Working with a timeline tends to help most people bring into play their visual thinking as well as connect everything they need to do so it looks like a unified plan, rather than a long burdensome list of to-dos or calendar dates. If you don't know how long something might take, just use your intuition and common sense to choose a time period. If you are committed to accomplishing your vision, then you will notice your mind finding ways to make it real within the time frame you set up. Having no time frame is like having no vision—you lose your way very easily. Specifically, you lose the cramming effect (uh-oh, this is due next week, and I've put it off for three months, so now I'd better at least give it a shot). You also lose the hypnotic effect (giving your mind an assignment so that it begins working on the task even when you're not conscious of it, including during sleep as so many geniuses have discovered). You also may just put off things until they can no longer occur.

The two timelines that follow show the stages of writing a book. The *level one timeline* shows the major steps, which include determining the exact topic, gathering a list of research materials to read, reading the materials, outlining the book, and so on. Some of the tasks occur during the same time period, such as doing research to find materials and beginning to read those materials. Other steps, such as writing the book, depend upon completing previous steps and are sequential on the timeline. For increased visual clarity you can use different colored bars or shadings to indicate each general phase of the project—in this case, gray for research steps, black for writing and editing, and white for steps relating to publishing. Those same colors or shadings can be used for the next step, the level two timeline.

The *level two timeline* expands a major goal or step from the level one timeline. That means each goal, each bar, on the first-level timeline becomes a new timeline, divided into its own steps shown by its own set of bars.

In the level two timeline example that follows, gathering a reading list for the book is divided into its four component steps—internet search, library search, bookstore search, and coming up with ideas through discussion with colleagues knowledgeable in the field. Of course, the time period for this level two timeline (January 15 to about March 1) corresponds to the time period for this same task on the level one timeline. Because the total time is less than two months, the timeline chart is broken down by weeks instead of by months as our hypothetical author is honing in on more specific tasks and dates. As you can see, she plans to talk about her topic with colleagues during the entire research phase. She also has divided the internet search into two phases, one at the beginning of research and another after the bookstore, catalog, and database searches are complete, figuring she might have some new leads for internet searching at that point.

Our author might then break down one of the level two steps into greater detail on a *level three timeline*. On that timeline, the goal of discussing ideas with colleagues might be divided into its components, such as meeting with individuals in the field, attending professional meetings, and making calls.

Once she has the timelines showing a given week of activities, she can divide these activities by day on a standard scheduling calendar, knowing exactly what she can do and needs to do today, the goal of the entire exercise.

Level 1 Timeline: Writing a Book

Tasks	Jan	Feb	Mar	Apr	May	Jun	Jul	Aug	Sep	Oct	Nov	Dec
Specify Topic	▓											
Gather Reading List	▓	▓										
Locate, Read Research		▓	▓									
Prepare Basic Outline				▓	▓							
Organize Notes					▓	▓						
Write Intro & End						▓	▓					
Write Chapters							▓	▓	▓			
Review—Editorial Board										▓	▓	
Make Corrections											▓	
Research Publishers		▯	▯	▯	▯	▯	▯	▯	▯	▯	▯	
Mail to Publishers												▯

Level 2 Timeline: Gather Reading List

TASKS	1/15–1/21	1/22–1/27	1/28–2/3	2/4–2/10	2/11–2/17	2/18–2/14	2/25–3/3
Internet Search	▓	▓				▓	▓
Library Search			▓	▓			
Bookstore Search			▓	▓	▓		
Discuss with Colleagues		▓	▓	▓	▓	▓	▓

Let's put what we have just learned about timelines into a step-by-step activity:

EXERCISE 14: Action Plan Timelines

Purpose

❑   To generate the first draft of an action plan using timelines

What You Need

❑   The Level One and Level Two Timeline Worksheets that follow the instructions or your own similar tables

❑   Paper for initial brainstorming

❑   Your lifework summary statement (LSS)

❑   Any other material about your vision you'd like to use as cues and reminders

❑   Pens or markers in a variety of colors

❑   45 minutes

What To Do (Part I)

1.   List every task you think you might need to do to accomplish your LSS or any goal that you chose based on your LSS. Don't worry about the order yet. If you have a number of distinct major lifework goals (for instance, becoming a motivational speaker and becoming a best-selling author), split these up and give each its own action plan and timeline.

2.   Review the list, and place a star by the major tasks.

3.   Determine the order of these starred tasks. You can do this by moving from first to last or by working backwards from your goal as explained in the previous section. Remember that some steps can be done simultaneously, and some can be done only in sequence. That's why we're using the bar graph form of timeline which shows both kinds of actions.

4.   List these tasks in order under the tasks column on the level one timeline worksheet that follows these directions.

5.   Write at the top of each remaining column the days, weeks, or months until you'll reach your goal. Use days if your goal will take two weeks or less. If your lifework goal will take two

months, label a column for each week. If it will take a year, use one column for each of the 12 months. If longer, use columns for each quarter.

6. As shown in the examples, draw a bar to indicate the start and completion date for each task you've listed in the first column. Have a bias toward doing things sooner rather than later when you have a choice. These dates may change as you learn more, but they will get you going.

Congratulations! You now have a basic action plan in the form of your level one timeline. Of course, it doesn't contain all the details you might need to explain each of the major steps or goals you listed. That information can go in your lifework journal or elsewhere. Timelines, like your mindmaps, aren't about explanations, but about key elements and their proper sequence.

Now you're ready to create your level two timelines. To select the end goals for these timelines, you'll begin by viewing each of the major tasks on the level one timeline to determine which will be appropriate end goals for level two timelines. If even more detail is needed, then the tasks listed on the level two timeline can become goals for level three timelines, and so on.

What To Do (Part Two)
1. Repeat all the steps from the part one directions to generate level two timelines. Put all these timelines on one worksheet if there's enough space.
2. If the level of detail is enough to plan your weeks and days, that may be all you need. If not, take each of the tasks on the level two timelines and make them end goals on their own level three timelines.
3. Continue to draw additional levels of timelines representing smaller and smaller tasks and time periods, until you are down to a goal you can accomplish in a week or two, at which point you may want to note them on a standard calendar or to-do list rather than a timeline.

Note: The timeline worksheets that follow may be too small or divided inappropriately to accommodate your particular needs. You may need only four columns or maybe 16 instead of the 12 shown. Rather than forcing your timeline onto the one shown here, draw your own using the ones that follow as models, or use any table making or project management software that you like to produce a customized timeline grid.

Worksheet: Level 1 Timeline

											TASKS

Worksheet: Level 2 Timeline

										TASKS

While you may wind up with a large number of timelines, depending on your vision, you don't need to keep all of them in front of you every day. All you usually need are timelines relating to what you need to do in the next day, week, and month. As things change and you reassess your progress, you will need to check the other timelines to see if they need adjustment, starting with the first level and working down. You also may not need to be very detailed about steps you will be taking well in the future, but do need to at least determine if you need to start work now on distant goals even though the completion date may be years away.

Having developed at least two levels of action plan timelines, let's not lose sight of their *fundamental purpose*, which is to help you determine what you need to do today, the only day you can actually do anything.

Doing something today is a vital component to lifework. I want to emphasize the importance of finding something to do now, even if it seems to stray a bit from the central work you must do. Momentum is critical. Remember Newton's First and Second Laws of Motion? Objects at rest tend to stay at rest and those in motion tend to stay in motion. The same, at least metaphorically, applies to most of us. Once we get stuck, many of us tend to stay stuck and find it hard to get going again, especially on a long-range plan. Most of us, once we get moving, tend to keep moving until some large "object" stops us. We need to keep moving. We need to keep up an inner sense of momentum and actual movement. That can only happen if you have steps to take on a regular basis, whether it's daily or weekly.

But what about when you're not sure what's the next best step or are waiting for someone else to complete something before you can take the next big step? This brings us to *Lang's Primary Lifework Principle*, which is: *There is always a next step you can take*. This means that you may not know exactly what would be best to do or what you ought to do. You may not be able to take the next step you'd like to take because you're legitimately waiting for something else to happen first. But there's always *something* you can do that will move things along.

You may say that there have been many times when you just didn't know what to do or found yourself doing things that were leading you astray. Then your next step might well be to admit it and go find help to determine what to do—whether that means going to a friend or colleague (see the next chapter on networks and resources) or the internet or a library or bookstore.[10]

And sometimes taking a step might mean just jumping in and doing something small and a little risky just to keep the juices flowing and the momentum going.

---

[10] If you don't know which book or internet site to start with for specific job-hunting topics, a good place to start is Richard Bolles' site, *jobhuntersbible.com*, which contains links to job search resources. The site is an adjunct to Bolles' classic career book, *What Color Is Your Parachute?* which comes out with current job-hunting information and resources in each year's edition.

Chapter 9. The Power of Networks

You'll probably find that you can't just move ahead step-by-step to your goal without some support or help from others. Birds are reportedly able to fly 70 percent further when in groups than when flying alone, and so too with people. That means you need a clear understanding of your community of support, or support networks.

Realize it or not, all of us already have extensive support networks, only we don't usually call them by that name. These are the people who give us emotional and spiritual support; offer ideas and advice; and introduce us to new people, new places to go, and new opportunities to learn and grow.

And that's a good start for thinking about your career support network because you can start with those people you already know. I prefer to think of them as a community of support rather than a network. When I think of network, I think about people tied to each other to trade services and favors. When I think of a community of support, I think about people helping each other to create a more rewarding and wholesome group and personal life. However, because networking is so common a term, we'll use it here to avoid any confusion.

Here are the categories of people you will most likely need over the long term:

- People who help hold you accountable for what you say you are going to do (see section on success partners below)
- People who have the information you need (including names of helpful contacts)
- People who can support you emotionally and spiritually
- People who can serve as advisors and as creative spurs
- People who can be mentors in a particular task, role, job, or career

EXERCISE 15: Network Overview

Purpose

❑ To help you recognize all the support you already have
❑ To make your network easily accessible
❑ To clarify who can help you with what kind of tasks

What You Need

❑ The Networking List Worksheet
❑ Pen or pencil
❑ 15 minutes initially. (Return to this exercise to keep adding names)

What To Do

1. Make a table with six columns or use the worksheet that follows these instructions.

2. The first column is for the names of all the people you know. The second column (SP) is for success partners. The third column (I) is for those who might have useful information or connections. The fourth column (E/S) is for those who might provide emotional and/or spiritual support. The fifth column (A) is for those who can provide you with useful advice. And the final column (M) is for everyone who might be able to mentor you in your chosen field.

3. In the first column, list the names of everyone you know. Begin by simply listing names of friends and family—including your children whatever their ages. Don't worry about the

order right now. Just keep adding names. If you don't come up with at least 50 people, you are either a hermit or aren't making a good-spirited effort. This is not a popularity contest, but a chance to see how many people you know who might be able to help you. These can include people from work, your next door neighbor, a favorite sales clerk, your mail carrier, a fellow swing dancer, and the person you smile at in the work cafeteria. While writing the names, don't even think about what role they might play in your lifework plan.

4. After writing all the names, place an X in *all* the columns that might apply strongly to each person on your list. Some people will be able to provide all five forms of assistance and others may not be able to help in any way (though this is rare if the person is an adult). Wait until the upcoming section on success partners to place X's in the SP column.

Worksheet: Networking List

NAME	SP	I	E/S	A	M

Worksheet: Networking List

NAME	SP	I	E/S	A	M

The most common concern I hear from those who haven't been effective in the past with such one-on-one networking is that they wouldn't want to really bother most of these people, so what good is it to include and mark off their names.

As with informational interviews, the problem is thinking that you would be bothering colleagues and friends if you seek their support. If your time is respected, how bothered are you if someone sincerely asks you for some advice or for the name of someone in a particular organization or someone in a particular career? Probably you feel good to be of service, to be considered worth asking, to be able to do a favor.

The big keys to succeeding in asking for help are:

- Being sincere in wanting help (You really would appreciate help and aren't asking for advice just to flatter or seek some unstated advantage.)
- Asking if what you want to talk about is okay
- Setting reasonable limits about the help you want (how much time it will take, etc.)
- Being willing to remain friendly even to someone who prefers not to help

The other big key is your willingness to help others. It's absolutely essential that you are as open and prepared to give support as you are to receive it. That means you are actively available as a resource for other people and are willing to make the time and commitment to help them in whatever ways that you can. This goes beyond simply trading time with friends or colleagues (you do an hour internet search for me and I'll advise you for an hour about how to start your own business). It's a spirit of making things happen for everyone. Put simply, it's about creating a generosity of spirit in yourself and your community. Minimally, this will generate personal and communal creativity in ways you can't now imagine.

Networking One on One—Success Partners

Career and executive coaches help individuals in many ways—asking the right questions at the right time, listening deeply, presenting ways to approach difficulties, helping to devise new frameworks, suggesting networking possibilities, creating ways to set up action plans or to clarify visions and goals—to name a few.

In addition, there's one vital function coaches perform just by being coaches—holding clients accountable. When you work with a coach, there's a day and time for your next coaching session, by which time you have agreed to complete certain, specific tasks that are part of a larger action plan. That simple fact has astonishing force. Suddenly things get done that had been merely haunting us from to-do lists.

You can also do this without a coach—with a friend or even by yourself. In fact, when I do career and lifework coaching, I always recommend that clients have someone to hold them accountable, a *success partner*, in addition to myself.

EXERCISE 16: Establishing Accountability

Purpose
❑ To keep up momentum in your lifework quest
❑ To help establish realistic deadlines and schedules
❑ To keep you on track
What You Need
❑ A friend or colleague or family member willing to help as explained below
❑ 5–10 minutes initially
What To Do
1. Choose someone you trust. Your partner should:
   • Be reliable in coming to meetings
   • Want you to succeed fully
   • Be able to keep accountability issues separate from other issues. (For example, spouses and significant others are

not always the best success partners. There can easily be confusing emotional spillover between relationship issues and work issues.)

2. Determine a regular schedule for your meetings. Most people find that every one to two weeks works out well. Just make sure it's enough to keep you moving along, but not so much you feel overwhelmed.

3. Make your meetings a high priority. Get to them on time. Set reasonable time limits for the meetings, and do your best to hold to them. How long is long enough? For basic success partner meetings, 10 minutes per person may be enough.

4. At your first meeting, determine
   • How long to meet each time
   • How often to meet
   • The tasks you will accomplish by the next meeting

5. Put those tasks in writing. Each of you should have a copy of your tasks and your partner's tasks.

6. At the next meeting, check in to see which of those tasks were completed. Keep this simple and direct. Go through each task on the list, and ask your partner if he or she completed it. If not, ask if it should be put on next session's list. Ask if there's anything you can do to support your partner in doing the task. If you wish, go from this simple 5-minute check-in to further discussion of what help each of you can provide the other in accomplishing goals. This is a bonus activity, so make sure you've first simply checked in, which is the purpose of the exercise.

7. Reward yourself. Choose whatever rewards seem appropriate for completing tasks on your list. At least as valuable as a reward is taking the time to recognize what you are getting done. We often focus on what we haven't completed, rather than appreciating how much we are getting done. On your to-do lists, have a column for completed tasks. Instead of tossing out the list when completed, check off what you've

completed, and review it after a month. You may be surprised at how much you've accomplished.

Success Partner Don'ts

1. Don't blame/shame/ridicule your partner or yourself for not completing tasks.
2. Don't get bogged down in analysis of "failure"—why you or your partner didn't get something done. These meetings are primarily about checking in. Analysis is an extra and is best applied to how to do something *now* rather than to why something didn't get done.
3. Don't overcommit. Be realistic about what you can get done, but keep some momentum going by doing something for each session.
4. Even if you want to do problem-solving work with each other, always complete your accountability meeting first.

If you follow these guidelines, your momentum and sense of accomplishment will build, you will find it less and less likely that you will feel stuck, and you and your success partner will continue to make steady progress toward your goals.

It's amazing what power this simple check-in has for many people. Perhaps it's just the guilty schoolchild within us that procrastinates on assignments (even when we assign ourselves the work) until they are due and someone sees what we have and haven't done. Perhaps it's just a matter of meeting stated commitments and agreements. In any case, I know my success partner and I often wind up rushing to finish our lists the day or two before our next meeting. Without the meeting the items would surely be put off.

Maintaining Momentum—Sampling

Meeting weekly or biweekly with your success partner is one way to keep up the momentum of your lifework process. It's another way of setting dates when things are to be finished and another way to obtain help in completing tasks and celebrating results, small and large.

Another useful tool is sampling. Sampling is anything you do that gives you an experience related to your vision and goals. It can be a volunteer opportunity in your field or a tour of a place you'd like to be or a course on something you need to learn, or a million other things so long as it lets you sample the life you are planning.

This serves two purposes. First, it lets you test out whether this is really the direction you want to take. For instance, if you want to do environmental training in the outdoors, you volunteer to assist someone who is doing just that at a nature center or wilderness area. This will let you in on some of the responsibilities and challenges and, hopefully, pleasures of that experience while giving you access to someone who can answer questions and serve as a model.

Second, sampling keeps you in contact with the direct experience of your dream. It's very difficult to stay on your path if it's a long one. You need to viscerally remember why you are doing all the work. I know that during the long Minnesota winter when I am not bicycling, I remember I liked cycling, but only when I actually go cycling again in the spring, do I reconnect with the exact experience that I love so well. It's as if I remember about it in images and thoughts, but the physical and emotional power of the experience has been lost. The same is true of any experience that is important to you that you don't do for a while, including activities related to your lifework.

EXERCISE 17: Planning a Sampling Experience

Wherever you are in your lifework process, you can devise sampling activities to help you test out your choices and renew your emotional and spiritual connection with your vision. Whether you are thinking of becoming a teacher or carpenter, engineer or tour guide, salesperson or acrobat, there are sampling activities just waiting for you to discover them.

Purpose
❑ To devise and participate in sampling

What You Need
❑ Your imagination
❑ Some idea of your lifework vision, what you may want to do
❑ 10 minutes to brainstorm/mindmap possibilities and however long it takes to do your sampling activities
❑ Pen and paper for initial brainstorming
❑ Potential Sampling Activities Worksheet

What To Do
1. Review your lifework summary statement and/or day log from your ideal life
2. Mindmap possible ways to participate in any of the tasks that make up the lifework vision expressed in your lifework summary statement or your day log. For instance, if you want to be a nurse, you can list taking a CPR course or volunteering at a hospital or getting permission to shadow a nurse as she goes about her activities or assist at a free clinic. If you want to open a B&B, you might (as one friend of mine has done) volunteer to work at one in exchange for learning the ropes. (This led to a part-time job which further educated my friend.) Or take a course on opening a B&B, or tour B&B's, or create a one-day B&B at your apartment or house, inviting over some friends to play guest roles while you act as if you are the owner.
3. Enlist the help of your network to obtain opportunities and, if needed, to think of possible activities. Even reading a

novel about a nurse or a biography about someone in the field you are interested in, can energize you again.

4. Once you have a list of sampling possibilities you like, begin to schedule the activities on a regular basis. It can be as little as one every few months if that keeps you connected. Or it can be more often.

5. If you are unsure of which direction to take, rate the opportunities on your new mind map according to how do-able they are. Use a 1–5 scale, with 5 as the most do-able. Rate them again according to which is most useful, also using a 1–5 scale. Add up the two numbers (the do-ability factor plus the useful factor) for each activity, and you will see which ones are overall most valuable according to these two criteria. Make them priorities and schedule at least one of them for the next week or two if at all possible.

Worksheet: Potential Sampling Activities

1.

2.

3.

4.

5.

6.

7.

Act Now. Action Is Learning

Author and management guru Tom Peters often uses the phrase, "Ready, Fire, Aim," switching the usual order to emphasize the importance of trying things out frequently and quickly in order to stay in business. That can mean bringing a new product to market or trying out a new way to improve customer service. Get ready and then fire. Once you've fired, you can best tell whether your attempt was in the right direction or not. If you take too much time aiming first, you will lose out to other competitors who will have fired more rapidly and fixed up their problems (re-aiming) before you even get off a shot.

What I like to tell lifework clients and class participants is something similar. If you aren't sure what to do, then do something, and you'll know much better whether it's what you should continue to do or not. Don't do something huge. Do something small. Frequently. Take lots of chances. But small ones. That's the fastest way to learn.

But don't forget about getting ready. While we don't want to slow ourselves down by trying to know the exact right course of action at each step, we do have to be prepared in larger ways. That's what much of this book is about—making sure you have done the ready in ready, fire, aim. Now is the time to fire. All the previous work here is a way of drawing back the bow so that you will get off a powerful shot aimed at a clearly defined target. Once it is drawn back, don't stand there in indecision and tension. Release the arrow.

Chapter 10. When Bad Things Happen to Good Plans

So you've answered the who, what, where questions and have come up with timelines and action plans and support networks. Everything is great. The world is beautiful. You're brilliant and your ideal future is on its way. Then it happens. One day, as you are following the steps of your action plan, you run into a brick wall. Something significant and unexpected happens. Your boss tells you your plan for shifting your role at work is impractical, the school with the courses you need just went bankrupt, the loan that seemed a no-brainer doesn't materialize, three informational interview prospects in a row told you your ideas are fantasy.

Now what?

First, take a deep breath. Get yourself centered. Then remember to draw on all the resources you have been developing.

There are your gifts and skills. It doesn't hurt to review the list of universal gifts and remember that you have shown persistence and courage in the face of difficulties before. You can do it again. It also helps to remember you have the particular skills needed to accomplish your dream, and wherever you need outside help, it is there. Review your community support list. Even if you don't actually call on anyone, it is good to recognize all the people who might help you out—with emotional support, informational support, or mentoring support.

Beyond this is your vision. Remember that lifework is a process more than a destination. Even if you achieve the exact vision you set out to achieve and are thrilled with what you've accomplished, it is in human nature to then want new challenges. We seek out higher levels of possibilities, so the vision isn't ever an end point. This means you are always on a lifework journey. Part of that journey will include downturns and disappointments, confusion, and unexpected difficulties. Learn how to accept and even enjoy the challenge of overcoming these obstacles. Learn how to learn from them. Learn how to laugh about them and yourself.

What about revisiting the vision? Often people start compromising their vision after a few setbacks. "It was a great vision, but I couldn't really bring it to life, so I'll try to do something I'm less passionate about." If you find yourself thinking that—stop! Although you may need to rethink your vision, most of the time you need to rethink your action plan and timelines and use creative means and support networks to find other ways of achieving your vision.

Let's say you needed funding to purchase business equipment to start an antique store but a bank loan didn't materialize for the equipment as you had planned. Instead of saying that's not possible—first, look for other ways to get the money you need. Perhaps you can borrow from someone in your support network, or better yet, make them an investor in your new business or plan. Or maybe you can find a partner. Maybe you need to earn more money in your current job until you have the money you need. Maybe you can start the business out of your home and/or on the internet or in a back room in someone else's furniture store.

However, if in trying everything you can think of to make your antique store a go, some different opportunities arise that excite you even more, don't just jump at it, but certainly consider it. Maybe someone says they've been interested in making customized furniture and want someone to sell their furniture, and you find that prospect interesting and believe it to be complementary to your antiques business. Of course look into it even though it may change your vision. Just keep checking back with your passions, gifts, skills, and lifework summary statement to make sure you aren't just jumping at the first opportunity.

Improving Your Thinking—How to Approach Adversity

Research psychologist Martin Seligman has nearly a half century of studies[11] showing that to succeed in new enterprises (and to be healthier, to be more popular, to live longer, and to improve your chances of winning elections and winning sports events) you need to respond to adversity by seeing possibilities. You need to believe you can affect your situation for the better. In short, you need to be optimistic. Those who are least successful in new enterprises often suffer from learned helplessness, believing they can't affect their situation. Learned helplessness is not much different from learned hopelessness. The fastest way to get into that state is to make one or more of three basic errors in your thinking:

1. Believing you are a flawed person because of a particular error or failure

2. Believing all areas of your life are going badly because of one problem or one area of your life going badly

3. Believing a problem will never and can never improve over time.

Seligman calls these errors of thought—making a mistake or problem personal (number 1) pervasive (number 2), and permanent (number 3).

Making it personal is saying something like, "I screwed up that interview because I'm such a complete idiot." Pervasive means you goof up a job interview and say to yourself something like, "See, *everything* is wrong with my life." Permanence means

---

[11] An excellent overview of his research and conclusions are in Seligman, *Learned Optimism*, (New York: A. A. Knopf, 1990).

you goof up the interview and say to yourself, "That's typical. I *always* mess up interviews" (or getting jobs). These ways of thinking, while appearing extreme on the page are very typical of first reactions for many of us, as I've found by asking my classes.

All, however, are based on the same error of thought—extreme generalization from a specific situation. Because you screwed up a job interview (or maybe even the fifth or sixth interview—assuming you screwed it up, which is often a faulty read on the situation to begin with) doesn't mean everything else in your life is disintegrating. It doesn't mean that you have always and will always make the same error in job interviews. And it certainly doesn't mean that you are a flawed human being (an idiot) who can't change because the flaw is who you are.

Of course, that's hard to see when you are feeling down, but you can begin to notice these thoughts *as they arise* (it takes practice but isn't difficult*)* and be able to step back from them. You can witness the thought going by rather than getting caught up in it. Simply creating that distance, that mental space, greatly decreases the power of such thoughts. They no longer are automatically accepted as truths, but are simply thoughts going by while you are feeling unhappy.

Once you notice these thoughts as they arise, you can also directly argue with them as Seligman suggests. Then when you have such a thought you argue against it just as you probably would if someone else had told you how you always screw up or what a bad person you are.

Knowing how you tend to overgeneralize and mentally attack yourself will help you deal with any adversity in your life. This simple action will not cure all ills. It will not substitute for professional help for those who find themselves depressed or frequently angry, for example, but I have seen it make a significant difference. Instead of thinking you're an idiot, perhaps you can begin to laugh at how idiotic somebody, including you, can act in spite of all your talents and intelligence and charm.

The Journal as Lifework Ally

Journals can do amazing things. I once almost fell out of my chair, literally, because of what I found myself writing and the burst of energy and excitement I was feeling doing a creative journaling exercise. I've been teaching journal writing programs for adults and youth for more than 20 years and have seen first hand how the journal can be a reliable and valuable aid for creativity, self-knowledge, emotional clearing, spiritual development, planning, and healing. During the past decade, medicine has begun to notice the value of journals as well. Articles in a variety of professional health care journals, including one in *The Journal of the American Medical Association,*[12] have reported on studies demonstrating the physical as well as emotional health benefits of journaling. And guess what? The journal can also help you pursue your lifework vision, as you'll find out in the following exercise.

Special note for those feeling overwhelmed by the idea of keeping a regular journal: As much as I love journaling and delight in extolling its benefits, I also know that there are some of you out there who may feel overwhelmed by an exercise that you do each week rather than do once and move on. If that describes you, relax. Read the following exercise just to see what it's about for future reference and move on without guilt.

For the rest of you, start with the next exercise and then find your own ways to keep a lifework journal to help keep you motivated in good and bad times.

---

[12] Smyth, Joshua M. et al. "Effects of Writing About Stressful Experiences on Symptom Reduction in Patients With Asthma or Rheumatoid Arthritis." *Journal of the American Medical Association* (April 1999): 1304-1309.

EXERCISE 18: The Lifework Journal

Purpose

☐ To keep track of your progress and challenges

☐ To keep track of and give a space and time for creative ideas

☐ To have a place to safely look at and express your feelings

☐ To create another ally/friend in your lifework journey

What You Need

☐ A notebook you are comfortable writing in (see below) and a pen—or you can use a computer

☐ 10 minutes per week minimum

What To Do

1. Get a notebook for your journal or start one on your computer. Journals can be beautifully bound small books of unlined paper or spiral notebooks with lined paper. They can be large or small, with colored paper or white paper, unlined or lined, thick or thin. What's best? That is solely up to you, as long as you get something you will use and put down honest thoughts and emotions, one that fits your lifestyle (that is, if you like to write on-the-go, the journal should be portable). You'll know whether or not you are comfortable.

2. Use the journal regularly in any or all of these ways:

   A. Do the exercises from this book in your journal.

   B. Brainstorm and keep track of any idea that comes to you that even *might* be related to helping you on your journey. Keep these ideas in their own section, with each idea having its own one- to three-word title (such as Getting Financed or New Product Idea) so you can easily locate it. Then review these ideas whenever you feel stuck. Even if you've read them before, the reading reconnects you with your more creative side and often reminds you of ideas you had forgotten or stimulates new ideas.

   C. Keep an Accomplishments Journal, as explained below:

      1. At the end of each day (or each week at the longest), keep track of every little thing you did to promote

your lifework process. This can be a list of a few words for each accomplishment. In an adjacent column, note in a few words how it felt doing and completing this task. This is not a list of big projects completed, like getting a degree in library science. It is a list of small to-dos that you did, such as purchasing a notebook and pen to do journaling or calling someone to arrange an informational interview.

2. At the end of each month review everything you've accomplished. Most people are surprised at how much they did. If you are disappointed, see if you can do more or if your expectations are unrealistic. Now is a good time to determine what you hope to accomplish next month.

Chapter 11: Frequently Asked Questions

Leading people through this lifework process, I've found that certain questions tend to come up most often. This chapter provides answers to a few of these important questions—ranging from the most practical about money and health to the most esoteric about psychology and spirituality.

What should I do if I don't have the money to follow my lifework dream now or maybe ever? Should I even look at my dreams if they might only frustrate me?

There are many variations on this question about lack of money. Some people know they need to get more education and have no savings for it. Others feel they are caught between going for their personal dreams and being responsible about saving for their children's future. Others already are in debt and believe they must stay in their current job so as not to increase their debt.

The answer for everyone is different in detail but the same in approach, which is this: Go through a lifework exploration process no matter where you are in your life. Find your lifework. Make a plan, even if it's a 25-year plan. The very process will probably unleash new ways to achieve your lifework vision that gets you out of the "it can never happen" mindset. It may also lead to many serendipitous meetings or opportunities as mentioned earlier. If you don't start working on it, there's even less chance of it happening. Of course, you have to be responsible with your financial needs and obligations. That doesn't mean you're stuck.

Second, make finances part of your vision, what you're hoping to achieve and not what's preventing you from getting ahead. Go back to your ideal day log and see what kind of income you'd need to live the life you've described. Your ideal day log roughly shows you at least some of what you really want materially. For instance, if in your day log you are living in log cabin in Montana you can determine what that would cost. You can expand on this 24-hour period to determine approximately what you will need financially to comfortably make your vision real. Then it can be part of your vision and part of your planning, rather than the obstacle that is keeping you from your vision and plans.

Thirdly, recognize you may need new ways to bring in money as well as a plan to achieve a new career. You may need to learn about investing, for instance. That can be one part of your action plan. You may need to restructure a debt or rethink how to pay for your own or your children's education. In other words, be creative in all areas of your life, not just in coming up with a lifework vision and plan.

The most important point is to get involved in the spiritual journey and passions of your life, rather than getting stuck in a passive, defeated view or only looking at the problems. Problems will always be there. So will new solutions. Look for them and recognize some things do take time. The point of this book is to help you get moving on the exciting journey of creating and fulfilling the vocational vision of your life. It's not about a certain amount of money or 100 percent success, but about keeping yourself spiritually alive by staying on track with your deepest passions, gifts, and values. Giving up because of money or any other factor is not a way to keep your spirit alive and flourishing. "Where there is no vision the people perish" (Proverbs). Don't give up your vision.

If I pursue my lifework and am committed to it, does that mean I will grow rich?

I find that if you are motivated to achieve your vision and are putting out a service or product with integrity, you are *more likely* to bring in money than someone seeking money by doing something they are bored doing. But that's no guarantee. Your values and your choice of lifework and lifestyle have a great deal to do with whether you become wealthy or not. For example, I don't know of too many poets who are wealthy from full-time work as poets, no matter how clear their vision, how deep their passion, how much integrity they show, and how wonderfully they write. Wealth also is very relative, and some people feel very wealthy with far less resources than other people who may not feel wealthy.

Money is essential in our world. Don't neglect it. Make it part of your vision. But it's not the main point of lifework, so don't look for guarantees about money or you may get off track.

Why aren't career tests part of the process you describe in creating a vision for your lifework?

I see tests as a minor element in the lifework process for most people. They can be useful the way all forms of input and feedback can be—by helping to stimulate understanding and new thinking. But how much more powerful, motivating, affirming, and creative is the insight that comes from doing your own inner work with the aid of people who know you. I've heard too many unhappy stories from people who come to me after taking various career and skills tests to believe they are a panacea or even an essential element in the lifework process.

Here's my own limited experience with such evaluations. When I was in college, I took a standard career inventory instrument designed to match my interests with the interests/profiles of people in a large number of careers. I was eager to receive the results. It turned out my highest match was with forest rangers. I had no interest then and continue to have no interest in being a forest ranger. The questionnaire was not completely absurd. I do love the outdoors and like to work independently and for all I know I have a great deal in common with the typical forest ranger. But none of that meant much when it came to what I wanted to do with my life. Oddly, in the past year, I told this story to a group of friends, and three of five present said they too had scored highest in the forest ranger category while in college (and we weren't all in college during the same years). As you might gather, none are forest rangers or anything close to it, and none are pining away to be forest rangers.

By contrast, a friend recently told me how career testing had proven extremely accurate in his case. He had taken a battery of tests while in high school. The psychologist administering the tests concluded this friend was very well suited to a career as physician, and more specifically as a research physician (rather than a clinical physician directly responsible for patient care). At the time, the friend dismissed the idea entirely. Today, this friend is indeed a successful physician involved in the research and development of medical products and is quite content with his profession. However, the tests had no traceable impact on his decision because he had completely forgotten about taking these tests when he decided on medicine as a career. His decision to go into research also emerged from his experiences, not the testing, which he didn't recall until reminded by his father years later. In other words, he went through his own learning and self-understanding process to discover for himself what he needed to do.

If you want to take tests, by all means, go take tests. They may or may not hold helpful results, as these anecdotes indicate. (If you do testing, it's best to discuss your results with a qualified professional who is open-minded as well as experienced in interpreting the tests.) Ultimately, the key point isn't whether tests may help or not. The key point is this: seek whatever assistance you need, but no matter what others say or tests indicate, your lifework vision and decisions must always be yours—something you believe in based on your deepest understanding of yourself, including your passions, skills, and values.

I've gone through your first three questions and exercises and have come up with so many things I love to do that I can't decide which to do. I can't commit to everything. Now what?

You do need to make some choices and not expect you will necessarily feel 100 percent certain of any decision. Staying stuck for months is not a strong place to be mentally, emotionally, or spiritually. Taking your time to decide is helpful *if* you are actively working on the issue and not just rehashing what you already know. The main action to take now is to look at what your life would be like if you pursued each of your choices. What would it be like is you worked at choice one or choice two? How would each affect your physical surroundings, your health, your family life, your social life, your wealth, your state of mind, and your sense of accomplishment? You may want to do an ideal day log exercise for each of the choices.

You may also see if some choices work best as hobbies and others as work. You might also ask yourself if there is there some way to combine a few choices into a single form of work—like transforming a love of skiing and a love of teaching into teaching skiing or writing educational articles about skiing.

Finally, look hard at your fears. Often we avoid choosing because we fear failure or looking stupid. Other times we may feel afraid because we don't know how to start doing something. These are relevant to the how question. How can you proceed to deal with the fear or consequences of "failure?" Fear is not the reason for deciding one lifework over another. Acknowledge the fear and keep moving. And don't let fear stop you from seeking appropriate professional help with the fear if you would benefit from it.

I am satisfied with my career choice but not really happy at work much of the time. I'm not sure why. I went through your lifework process and kept coming to the conclusion that I want to keep doing what I am now doing. Have I done something wrong?

Your conclusion is a common and often very affirming and welcome one. You are most of the way there. But if you're not basically feeling satisfied, you still need to identify what's not ideal about your particular circumstances. It's not the first two questions—who or what—that need more study, but the third question, the where question.

Unhappy at work, a nurse in one of my programs thought she needed a new career. She soon realized she still loved nursing, but was unhappy with her work in a hospital. She researched alternatives and discovered she would be more fulfilled in a clinic setting. She didn't need to change her lifework choice, only where and how she was doing it.

What does it look like when you are doing your lifework most ideally? Imagine you were in charge of your workplace and had the money and personnel to do just what you wanted. How might you reshape it? Once you answer that, you may have a better sense of what's missing or what's too stressful in your current situation.

I'm 64 years old and about to retire with an adequate pension. Will this process help me or is it only for younger people?

I believe we all need to regularly revisit our lifework vision and compare it with our lives to see if we are on track, given new circumstances in our lives and new interests and passions within us. Most people I talk with who are retired say they are looking for ways to continue to live a meaningful, satisfying life. That may or may not mean work activities in the most traditional sense. But the process to discover what you want to do during this phase of your life is the same and just as important. Keeping involved in family and community and remaining active mentally and physically are essential to a satisfying retirement and to staying healthy.

Maybe now is the time to complete an education, pursue volunteer work, write a memoir, share your skills as a mentor, be the kind of grandfather you wished you had, or sail the world. I've had more and more retirees showing up for my workshops lately. They understand the need to find rewarding activity and have the skills to do what they want. One retired man wanted to finally pursue his love of history. During the class, he identified this desire and went to a county fair where he saw an exhibit about local history and was able to sign up to join the history group sponsoring the exhibit. It might seem a small step to someone else, but his excitement in telling the story motivated all of us and showed how important a step it was to him.

I knew what I wanted to do and was doing it until health conditions stopped me. I can't pursue my lifework any longer. Do I need to accept something I am not passionate about?

That's always a painful question for me to hear. One woman on a call-in show told me her passion was farming. She had always loved animals and wanted to be a farmer. She had realized her vision in rural Minnesota, but health conditions prevented her from continuing the one thing she always knew she wanted to do. There's no easy answer when our dreams seem to fall apart. Chronic illnesses are in themselves difficult challenges and become even more difficult when they interfere with what we most love to do.

Of course, we have to deal with the grief we may feel from losing something we deeply love to do. We may seek the help and support of others, relying as well on our faith and sustaining beliefs.

And we learn to move ahead. Shifting the perspective from defeat to opportunity, even as a mental game, might open up new possibilities. We can look at other activities that we like to do. Maybe there's some underused parts of us that can be applied to an entirely new career. Going through the four questions of the lifework process can open up that opportunity.

There also may be new ways to approach a current passion. Instead of farming, maybe writing about farming or teaching something about farming or going to classes in the city to talk to children about animals or farming. These may not meet some of the basic original passions (being with the animals, for instance), but they may satisfy other interests. Often it's a crisis that brings out deeper qualities within us and raises our lives to a new level of meaning and reward.

How is this program different from goal setting as most people practice it?

Coming up with timelines and an action plan to reach your vision is a form of goal setting. What's different is that the goals come out of a vision which comes out of a search into your values, passions, and skills. This ensures that your goals relate to your vision. Using any particular technique to create an action plan and to set goals is much less important than knowing where you're going and having a plan based on that vision.

Some books on spirituality talk about not getting attached to one's desires, goals, and passions. And some books on spirituality refer to the need to quell desires and passions. How does your approach relate to these ideas? Can we be passionate and nonattached?

I don't find any contradiction between nonattachment and complete attention to one's deepest passions. The vision and the techniques in this program are just helpers to keep you on a spiritual path that connects your inner spiritual source with your outer actions in the world. They are not the source of fulfillment in themselves, so of course we do not want to be attached to them.

This can get a bit esoteric. My own view is that we need to do inner and outer work. The inner work is about laying the foundation for outer work, about making the connection with a universal spiritual source. Ultimate peace and fulfillment comes from an ultimate source and acting from that connection, not from a particular achievement or result. That ultimate source may be understood as God, the Divine, the Absolute, Pure Emptiness, or the Transcendent. Our outer work is about expressing that inner connection and knowledge in the world. That outer work is about fulfilling our unique roles. To me, that's lifework.

Some of the key ways to determine one's outer work are to learn about one's deepest passions, values, and gifts. Being passionate about something and having a vision doesn't mean we are attached to the vision or the passion, necessarily. We are guided by them as part of the journey, not attached to them as our source of spiritual fulfillment. Passionate, yet not attached. It's an apparent paradox, but one that we can learn about by acting upon it.

This lifework process is focused on finding what suits ourselves as individuals, our passions and values. Doesn't this contradict the idea of service and being helpful to others?

It may seem paradoxical to start with our individual drives and values and expect beneficial actions for others. Yet it works. I find that the overwhelming number of people willing to work through this process have a strong desire to feel useful and to be useful. It seems to be an almost universal passion. Similarly, helping others comes up as a top-ranked value for most people.

We could start with ideas of service instead of starting with personal passions, gifts, and values. What tends to happen, though, is that we look at all the helpful actions that are wonderful to do but seem painful or difficult to us, as if service must be opposed to personal fulfillment to be service. We are likely to look at what great people have done, rather than understand our own unique contributions. We may begin to lead other people's lives, not our own. It is very difficult to sustain an effort that is painful just because we can mentally identify it as good. I think it's valuable to stretch ourselves and go beyond our everyday comfort zone at times, but this doesn't mean we should take on a career or major activity that we cannot sustain except by forcing ourselves to continue.

By contrast, when we start with passions, values, and gifts, we are more likely to act from a sense of harmony and integrity within ourselves. That means we are more likely to come from the heart where we can connect with others most easily rather than an abstract idea of good which might increase our emotional and spiritual distance from others. Starting with our passions, we are more likely to continue our work over the long term because it's rewarding to us as well as others. Of course, this is just one approach to this complex topic. Each person needs to find whatever process is in accord with his or her values and beliefs.

Chapter 12: Endings and Beginnings

You've reached the end of this book, and if you've read it all and completed all of the exercises—congratulations—you have come a very long way. You have answered the four key questions. You have drawn timelines and learned about lifelines. You've imagined your ideal life and devised lifework and core statements and action plans. You have learned how to use creativity techniques you can return to when you need them. You have a defined network of support, including a success partner.

Now might be a good time to check back on the three goals (and your dream goal) that you wrote down while reading the first chapter. How many of those goals have you accomplished, and how many others have you accomplished that you didn't even think about back then?

If you haven't completed all the exercises in the book, that's fine too. You may not need all of them. You may be great at developing action plans and used this book to help you clarify your vision. Or you may have read to this point while continuing to work on the who question or your values or action plan. There's no timetable for completing any activity in this book except the one that you decide is right for you. There's no right place to be on your lifework journey, except the place that keeps you creatively moving ahead.

No matter where you are, I hope you take time now to notice all that you've done and all that you've learned. Find some new way to celebrate who you are and what you've done. Reward yourself. Invite others to help you in your celebration.

At the end of my workshops I usually ask people what they have learned that has the most value for them or what has affected them most profoundly. As you can imagine, the answers vary greatly. Many talk about having a path to follow or a vision to inspire them. Others emphasize the sense of community they realize they have in their lives to help them. Others focus more on how they've learned to use their values in their everyday lives. Some have realized how passionate they are or how they've become more confident. Others are just excited to get moving again. As a final exercise, take a moment now to think what have been the three most valuable things you've gained from working with this book.

Endings also imply the need for new beginnings—next stages and next projects. What's next for you? Where are you headed? How can you best continue your lifework process? Only you can say, but here are three basic ideas to keep you going.

First: Realize you now have the basic skills, knowledge, and tools to succeed. You also have a network of support to help you find the resources you need when you don't know exactly what to do or where to turn. You know the questions you need to be able to answer. You have written statements to remind you of your purpose and passions. You know what your vision is or at least how to define a vision that will motivate and guide you. You have an action plan and timetables.

Second: Keep taking steps. Don't allow yourself to get so stuck that you do nothing. Remember there's always some useful step to take even if you're not sure of what the best step is. Remember how to be optimistic. If you need a jumpstart, return to your mindmaps, core statements, ideal day log, or your network of support. If you feel lost about your goals, look at your lifework summary statement to see if you are still on track. Redo the exercises as needed or do them for the first time. Keep meeting with your success partner.

Third: Enjoy the journey. Enjoy wherever you are, whether still finding patterns in your passions or completing the last step in your action plan. Achieving a vision is a splendid accomplishment. But once you complete a vision, you'll have a new or expanded vision, while the process of discovery and of working toward a vision continues and defines the way you spend much of your life. This process of moving toward your vision *is* your lifework journey, so take the time to savor wherever you are.

Famed United States Supreme Court Justice Oliver Wendell Holmes stated early in his life, "I find the great thing in this world is not so much where we stand, as in what direction we are moving." This book has led you through a step-by-step lifework process to stop drifting along aimlessly in no direction or going too slowly forward or in the wrong direction and to start moving effectively in a meaningful and fulfilling direction, no matter where you were standing at the start.

The process was less about finding the right career or retirement once and for all and more about constantly creating new ways to express your deepest passions, gifts, and values for the benefit of others. It was less about learning a particular system or exercise and more about consciously engaging in an ongoing adventure of body, heart, mind, and spirit. It was less about how others have succeeded and more about your unique path, your self-discovery, and your decisive actions.

Your lifework journey did not begin with this book, and it certainly doesn't end with it, either. There may or may not be a limit to the wealth and fame you achieve, but whatever obstacles you run into, there is certainly no limit to how much you can learn about yourself and how vital, fulfilling, and joyful your life can be. But don't take my word for it. Go out and realize your own vision, and see what you discover along the way.

About the Author

With activities ranging from mindmapping to swing dancing, Leonard Lang, Ph.D., presents ways to bring creativity, innovation, and spirituality into people's lives, workplaces, and organizations. A motivational speaker, coach, and trainer, Leonard has led programs for career coaches, facilitators, managers, ministers, nurses, physicians, teachers, writers, and teens. He has presented at the annual International Association of Facilitators conference and taught lifework programs at the Minnesota Career Development Association's annual conferences and at such educational institutions as the University of St. Thomas, University of Wisconsin, and Normandale Community College. He has edited *Home Words*, a book of writing by homeless people. His poetry has appeared in such literary journals as *Cimarron Review*, *The Journal*, and *Visions-International* as well as a national best-of-year poetry anthology, and for five years his book reviews were heard twice monthly on Minnesota Public Radio.

For information about lifework coaching or to arrange for a creativity or lifework program, please contact the author at:
Email: llang@writerscollective.org *or* llang@beardavenue.com
Phone: 612-925-5478